I0006834

the digital incunabula: rock • paper • pixels

the transition from analogue to digital

Patrick Aievoli

Zea Books
Lincoln, Nebraska
2015

Copyright © 2015 Patrick Aievoli.
All rights reserved.

ISBN 978-1-60962-076-9 paperback
ISBN 978-1-60962-077-6 ebook

Zea Books are published by
the University of Nebraska–Lincoln Libraries

Electronic (pdf) ebook edition available online at
http://digitalcommons.unl.edu/zeabook/

Print edition can be ordered from Lulu.com, at
http://www.lulu.com/spotlight/unllib

Dedicated to
Adele, Allison and Philip

Preface

This book started out as a presentation I gave at an Honors and Merit Fellowship Conference at LIU Post for Dr. Joan Digby, Director of the Honors College. Joan has been a true friend for over 15 years.

The purpose of that presentation, and now this book, is to discuss the similarities and differences that occurred via the overall desire to communicate through "whatever means necessary" - be it petroglyphs, ink or now pixels. The prior incunabulum and this new one are discussed: via recorded history, personal experiences and the beliefs of some experts who have presented their positions on the crisis, opportunities, and adjustments needed especially now in this new Digital Incunabula.

The people who can use this book are any educators, counselors, parents or students who are looking for information towards design or media as a future. The question asked at the end of this book is:

"If you were advising a child on their future in the design or media fields what would you tell them?"

Then the question becomes more personal.

"If you were advising YOUR child on their future in the design or media fields what would you tell them?"

Paola Antonelli in an interview states, *"In truth, design has spread like gas to almost all facets of human activity, from science and education to politics and policymaking. For a simple reason: one of design's most fundamental tasks is to help people deal with change."*

The reason for choosing design as the focus is based on Antonelli's quote; because everything funnels through design in its route to society whether: information, print, promotion, entertainment, education, or the arts.

Table of Contents

Chapter 1 - The first time

The first incunabulum is defined as:

a book printed before 1501 or any early period of invention

According to many sources, Gutenberg's invention of the modern printing press opened up the world to the age of the Renaissance and the Enlightenment through the spread of knowledge via books.

> *"Prior to the rise of the Internet, no innovation did more for the spread and democratization of knowledge than Johannes Gutenberg's printing press. Developed around 1440 in Mainz, Germany, Gutenberg's machine improved on already existing presses through the use of a mould that allowed for the rapid production of lead alloy type pieces. This assembly line method of copying books enabled a single printing press to create as many as 3,600 pages per day. By 1500 over 1,000 Gutenberg presses were operating in Europe, and by 1600 they had created over 200 million new books. The printing press not only made books affordable for the lower classes, but it helped spark the Age of Enlightenment and facilitated the spread of new and often controversial ideas. In 1518 followers of the German monk Martin Luther used the printing press to copy and disseminate his seminal work "The Ninety-Five Theses", which jumpstarted the Protestant Reformation and spurred conflicts like the Thirty Years' War (1618-48). The printing press proved so influential in prompting revolutions, religious upheaval, and scientific thought that Mark Twain would later write, "What the world is today, good and bad, it owes to Gutenberg." -*
> *http://www.history.com/news/history-lists/11-innovations-that-changed-history*

So denying this sequence or relative connection seems a bit odd, and in my opinion, so does the denial of the changes created from what some (including myself) wish to call the Digital Incunabula. So many disruptions have come about from the advent of this new means of communicating, archiving, and distribution that I liken it to a large stone being thrown into a pond. The closest ripples have the most power but the ones that reach out to the edge seem to have the greatest impact.

While discussing impact I have asked my students to respond to the question of which has had a greater impact - the printing press or the Internet?

Below are some of their responses.

"As anyone could acknowledge after reading this paper, the Internet has affected our society immensely. Although I did not go into detail with the impact of the printing press, I believe that discussion only needs to be at a minimum. Primarily because of the information I have provided speaks for itself and the printing press I think only caused a slight disruption in comparison to the Internet. Not to mention the printing press created more employment than it took away."

- Alecia Weiterschan - October 13, 2014

"The Internet, like the development of the printing press, can easily be pointed out as both changing history immensely. Like the printing press, the Internet disseminates information, but this time on a grander scale. Again, like the printing press, the Internet offers freedoms of privacy of thought. With the Internet, we each have our own printing press that spreads knowledge. We've cut out the middleman and allowed our society to attain information even quicker. The amount of information and the speed of access are astronomical and global. In an instant we can have whatever information we need at our fingertips. Allowing immediate feedback, the Internet entices the user in a different way than ever before. It may appear that the Internet had a greater impact simply just because of the global reach it has alone, however the Internet only started because of the printing press. The demand for knowledge to spread quicker developed only because of it original origins. Despite how quickly we can attain information now I feel the impact is harder to determine on the Internet more than the printing. By separating the impacts of the printing press and the Internet into economy, education, society, and so on--I believe it is still hard to take one stance over another. On a side note, if we are to look at what had more positives and negatives, I feel that the Internet is the winner with negative impact. The Internet has hurt a lot of creativity and hurts society more than it helps in some instances.

- Sequoyah Wharton - October 9, 2014

Here are some facts concerning the first incunabula and what I am calling the "Digital Incunabula".

The first incunabulum was before 1501:

- 1500–1000 printing presses were in operation throughout Western Europe and had produced 8 million books – E.L. Einsenstein

- In the Americas, the first extra-European print shop was founded in **Mexico City** in 1544 (1539?), and soon after **Jesuits** started operating the first printing press in Asia (**Goa**, 1556)

- In the 16th century tenfold, to between 15 and 20 million - Febvre

Now the Digital Incunabula (I propose) was from after 1450 and before 1962:

- 1962 - J.C.R. Licklider writes memos about his Intergalactic Network concept of networked computers and becomes the first head of the computer research program at ARPA

- 1964-67 - The Rand Corporation's Paul Baran develops message blocks in the U.S. while Donald Watts Davies, at the National Physical Laboratory in Britain, simultaneously creates a similar technology called packet-switching. The technology revolutionizes data communications.

- 1967 - Directing ARPA's computer research program, Robert Taylor initiates the ARPAnet project, which is the foundation for today's Internet

- 1968 - UCLA team sends first data packets

- 1971 - Ray Tomlinson sent the first e-mail message

- 1974 - Vint Cerf and Robert Kahn publish "A Protocol for Packet Network Interconnection", which specifies in detail the design of a Transmission Control Program (TCP) and coins the term "Internet" for the first time

- 1984 - The first email arrives in Germany from the U.S. on August 3, 1984. "Willkommen CSNET," it says. Werner Zorn plays a critical role in this event and establishing the German Internet. - http://www.internethalloffame.org/internet-history/timeline

- Around 40% of the world's population has an Internet connection today; in 1995, it was less than 1%

- The number of Internet users has increased tenfold from 1999 to 2013

- The **first billion** Internet users was reached in 2005

- The **second billion** Internet users was reached in 2010

- The **third billion** Internet users was reached in 2014 - http://www.internetlivestats.com/internet-users/

Some 50 years after the invention of the Internet, it has now grown to have over three billion people online with countless websites and millions of online journals. Comparing this event to the dawn of print... it's incredible to realize it took over 500 years for a similar effect to happen.

But what are the ripple effects from this Digital Incunabula? What kind of effect have those ripples had on the world? Are the effects malevolent or benevolent? As with anything there are parts of both involved with these disruptions. Again, it's for these reasons why I focus on the use and study of Design as it is, because this is the means by which the new information and interaction is deployed.

The first areas of discussion will be those that I personally am very familiar with - design and specifically printing. I have been in these fields since 1978 and have ridden the ups and downs of the advent of new technologies.

Chapter 2 - This time again

As a definition of the Digital Incunabula I offer this simple response.

The Digital Incunabula is the time from after 1450 to before 1962 when the Internet, and in essence, the personal computer were first made a possibility.

According to the Computer History Museum in Boston –

"This Internet Timeline begins in 1962, before the word 'Internet' is invented. The world's 10,000 computers are primitive, although they cost hundreds of thousands of dollars. They have only a few thousand words of magnetic core memory, and programming them is far from easy.

Domestically, data communication over the phone lines is an AT&T monopoly. The 'Picturephone' of 1939, shown again at the New York World's Fair in 1964, is still AT&T's answer to the future of worldwide communications.

But the four-year old Advanced Research Projects Agency (ARPA) of the U.S. Department of Defense, a future-oriented funder of 'high-risk, high-gain' research, lays the groundwork for what becomes the ARPANET and, much later, the Internet."

http://www.computerhistory.org/internet_history/

Schumpeter x Moore x Cerf = Digital Disruption

I am not an economist, a computer scientist nor a historian of any certifiable nature. What I am is old. I have been working in this space for close to 30 years. And with only that little bit of experience as my guide here is my take.

Schumpeter's Creative Destruction is an economic premise where new advances create destruction of old technologies and hopefully bring new possibilities. The difference is those advancements had years to slowly migrate into the current economy.

Now Moore's Law (Gordon Moore – founder of Intel) predicted that technology would double every 18 months. Dr. Moore debates the strict timeline as being his quote but never the less we all get the idea. And it has actually now sped up to technology doubling every two to three months.

Times all of this by another small innovation - the Internet (developed by many but usually the name Vint Cerf comes to the forefront here) and you can start to get a handle on why these times are so much more volatile.

New business models are created that are technology rooted and delivered by wireless global communication system. It appears to me to be like a meteor flashing through the sky at night. We all saw it and we all were amazed but only some had the wherewithal to follow the object and see where it landed. New fertile ground with huge potential - some will know what grows here and some won't.

I read a great quote from an article in TechCrunch.com the other day. Here are some amazing facts about this new economy.

> *"In 2015 Uber, the world's largest taxi-company owns no vehicles, Facebook the world's most popular media owner creates no content, Alibaba, the most valuable retailer has no inventory and Airbnb the world's largest accommodation provider owns no real estate."*

If this doesn't prove the strangeness of this new economy what does? It is pure disruption – crowd sourcing, social commerce, and divested industries - and at every level design and media have to understand how to speak to and speak through this new maze. It's all about the interface and the user experience design that makes for the success. And please note this is not an easy task. And this is why I am speaking through design.

Y Design?

The focus so far has been on design. The question is why chose design? What does design invoke that makes it so important? For years design has been seen as an ornamental choice. The right typeface, the right color, the right proportions - have these choices really made any difference? Probably not but today design has transcended that previous criteria. Today design has moved forward to actually interphase with and determine our choices in all things.

Today when you see someone walking around head tilted down staring at that small screen they are absorbing information, some of it necessary some of it discretionary. But how they absorb is the basis of all design choices today. It is called Interaction Design and it is created not by one, but by many - each stakeholder – user, designer and producer has credence. Each one has a significant part in how something is designed and why each piece got the importance it received.

Imagine creating a compass from a simple piece of metal and a thread of silk. You charge the metal with the silk by stroking it in one direction. Then once the metal is charged you place it on a floating leaf - a movable base - that helps point the newly charged metal - now a needle to true north. This is interaction design. The metal is your message, the silk the empirical knowledge base and the leaf the ability to grow, change and shift with the power of true north.

As we create design objects for this new millennium we need to make them malleable to the movement of the user. As the user shifts the object needs to follow that shift and point to true north. As society moves forward true north stays but their path changes based on the obstacles in their way. Our job as designers is to keep them on true north.

The problem is that any platform not malleable, not shift capable, not able to change direction towards true north effortlessly – like the floating leaf - tends to force the needle to point towards its knowledge base and conform to those limitations. Today that model has become extinct because it has lost its ability to find its way. No compass – no future.

My early experience in the world of design and printing

I have been involved in the print industry since 1978. My first job was with a small print house/newspaper company in Lawrence, NY. It was family-owned and had a very small web press and some sheet-fed units. On my very first day, taking my very first steps into the plant through the back doors, I heard a scream and the presses slam shut. A press assistant had just caught his hand in the end rollers on the web press and his fingers were smashed. It was like that scene in "Field of Dreams" where Midnight Graham took a step off of the ball field and aged 60 years to go back to being Doc Graham. I kind of watched my whole life go before my eyes and realized instantly this was not for me. But what else could a young designer do for a job?

It was a great re-education. I learned all the fundamentals of designing ads and editorial; spec'ing type and setting it to shooting stats; making film, developing negatives, opaquing them and burning plates to put out for the pressmen to bend and run on press. It was an instant education and I was getting paid to learn; it was extremely worthwhile. I learned a few simple lessons I have kept with me my whole life. If you want it quick, cheap and good – pick two and call me back. And the good news is – you only have one mistake. The bad news – you have 10,000 copies of it. Print media was a very tough boss.

I was introduced first to digital machines in 1974 – the Compugraphic typesetting system. It was half analog and half computer. Type and - also amazingly - rule lines or boxes could be typeset electronically. My years of fighting with the ruling pen and rapidograph pens just disappeared before my eyes.

On the day I was introduced to my first Macintosh computer, in 1986 at McGraw Hill, my life changed once again. This time it lead to a major technology shift, and now almost 30 years later I look back and wonder what would have happened had I not been selected to try this new technology? Where would these ripples have placed me? What would have happened if I did not embrace this new means to an end? I had worked for 6 years to finally get into a reputable company in a reputable field – educational publishing. However, now I was faced with even a bigger challenge. It was sitting in a large box with a big multicolored apple on it, and I had no idea what was next.

Well what *was next* was a new place. A place I should have been in a decade before - in front of a classroom. It was the absolute best move I could have made in all my life.

What class is this?

I have been fortunate to teach students from freshman to graduate level over the last 27 years, everything from 2D design to Interaction Design theory and practice. The one example of my teaching style that has stayed in my mind happened one day in freshmen 2D design class. It was the first day of class, and for these students, the first day of college. I bound in and simply started lecturing about the virtues of design, how it's everywhere, and how it affects everything we do as a society. I dove into references and examples from the chair they were sitting in to the laptop they use and the games they play. Everything has been designed with a purpose by somebody who sat in chairs just like they did on their first day of school. I continued to tell them how they should never stop learning, that it's important to focus in every class they take, and how knowledge and logic will be their wheelhouse and toolkit. This lecture continued for over an hour. I was feeling pretty good about the lecture, like I had really done my job to educate. Then, from out of the corner of my eye, I see a little hand come up from a very young-looking, dark-haired girl.

I ask, "Yes, how can I help you?"

The reply, "What class is this?"

The really funny part of this story is that she went on to my graduate program, and now is the Senior Mobile Design Manager for the largest retailer in the United States. Her design work is responsible for generating literally billions of dollars in revenue for that company. Fortunately and proudly I can say she is one of many.

Going Digital and Interactive

Since 1986, I had been looking for someone who saw the innovations I had witnessed at McGraw-Hill. I was fortunate enough to witness those transformations first hand and believed I was privy to a very big change. I really had no one to talk to about it, except for my mentor Cesare DelVaglio. Skip, as everybody called him, was the director of Electronic Publishing for all of McGraw-Hill. I met him inadvertently in 1986 and we are still friends today. Skip's family was in the printing business for a very long time. To this day he runs a printing company - even after leaving McGraw-Hill. I'm not sure where I'd be today if it wasn't for him. Skip opened the doors to a world of which I was just lucky enough to be a part. We called his work area 'Cesare's Palace', for it made sense.

Just as recently as August 2015 McGraw-Hill is still making strides towards Cesare's original goals of taking them digital. McGraw Hill Education CEO David Levin just published an article on HuffingtonPost.com entitled "Dear Students and Faculty: Please Go Digital". In this article he espouses the virtues of a digital publication – not simply an eBook format but a truly interactive learning product.

"The problem with print - and the digital opportunity
Print has been an effective way of sharing information since the time of Gutenberg, but it simply hasn't kept pace with the opportunities and demands of teaching and learning today. Of course, merely moving content from the print world to the digital ecosystem won't make a difference on its own. But by combining digital content with software that harnesses the science of learning - essentially, how the mind masters new concepts - we can work with faculty to create experiences that make learning more effective and efficient. These types of technologies go far beyond what's offered in an e-book, making learning entirely richer and more personalized. While it seems like this package would come at great expense, it's actually available today for roughly half the price of print." -
http://www.huffingtonpost.com/david-levin/dear-students-and-faculty_b_7957508.html

After leaving McGraw-Hill and starting my academic career, I was fortunate again to be asked by the Long Island Advertising Club (LIAClub) to speak at a conference in 1993. The topic I selected was "Multimedia". I was given a room and was asked to pick a panel. I chose some local industry friends and tried to moderate. When it was my time to speak, I opened with a bold statement. "In 5 years, half of your print budget will go to this new world called multimedia". I was almost thrown out of the room.

I had spoken of this many times in class as well, sometimes in continuing education classes with print industry people in the class. They stood up on chairs and screamed at me as I hit "Make Separations" on the computer and four sheets of paper came out of the laser printer. Each piece of paper represented an ink color perfectly separated and with registration marks. Only one printer, brave enough to see what was happening, took the sheets and brought them back the next week; he had transferred the paper to printing film and announced that they worked. He could print from them. The room got real quiet. A major disruption was starting and this time everyone in that room felt the shake.

Right after I had finished the LIAClub presentation, a gentleman my age came up to me and introduced himself. His name was also Pat, and he had seen the future as well. Now this is where it gets real weird. We both shared the same vision of the future for this digital age. We both had sons, both born in December during the same year. Both of our wives were pregnant and due at the same time in July. Yep, and both newborns were daughters. Our wives were Italian-Irish and both smarter than us. So of course we started working together and built our first prototype CD-ROM for a major retailer.

Now it gets *really* weird – we decided to take a trip to MacWorld'93. It was being held in Boston, which is about 5 hours from Long Island. We drove and talked quite a bit during the long drive. I asked him what his family did for a living. He told me they owned a couple of businesses - with one being a hair salon in a local shopping center – the biggest one on Long Island at the time. I remarked that so did an old college friend of mine. I described the hair salon, and you guessed it. I had gone to college (twenty years before) with his sister (a close friend). We screamed at each other while driving like David Spade and Chris Farley in "Tommy Boy". True story – great minds do think alike – even if it takes two decades.

After some time, we had a meeting with four other people; two of which were my students and two were business associates. There were six of us in a room, and each one had brought one person resulting in three groups of two. What's peculiar about this situation was that Pat brought Pat, Mark brought Marc, and Larry brought Larry. Like binary code we each brought our counterpart! It hasn't really straightened out since.

That gentleman has owned and operated a now large digital marketing firm for the past twenty-two years. All pretty much based off of that conference and MacWorld'93.

After that conference, a business associate who wanted to delve into the digital field from his existing print business also approached me. He had the funding and facilities to get a start up going and he wanted me to consult for it.

Working with students has been a true joy of mine and a major part of the story - you know the old adage, "Those that can – do and those that can't – teach". Well, I do agree with that to a point. So during the last 30 years I have always tried to keep one hand in the field by consulting. One of the major journeys along that way was a start up - Digital Interactive, or DI as we called it.

Being Digital - Interactive

At this very strange time and place I was able to gather together a truly wonderful group of my current and ex-students. I picked the best – Janice, Larry (yep same guy), Joe, and Rich. With the funding and facilities being provided by the two older print people and their son as COO, we started out on a very strange journey that brought us from 1993 to 1997, and included the board rooms and conferences of some very big names in all of the sectors we will speak about. During a very short window of time – just four years – we generated over $650,000 in revenue. Not a big number, but when you realize many start ups are revenue negative for the first five years... *plus*, we basically had to explain to every client what the hell we were talking about, you can begin to see how big of a deal this really was.

At the end of each industry sector I will give you a little section about those experiences from a first hand vantage point, using the abbreviation PA-DI for each.

That experience has taught me that changing your thinking from the "how" to the "why" to me is the essence of design in the 21st century. We are no longer a fringe non-essential part of the process like choosing between khaki and beige. Now, design is an integral part of the user experience. Now, the way in which we interact with objects - both physical and digital - is designed. Today, design has been brought to the forefront of economics, education, information, entertainment, and the arts. It was a journey into very unchartered territory that gave me my best education.

The main reason for telling these personal anecdotes is so you understand that I was involved in this process first-hand for over three decades and witnessed the transition from the inside out. I had friends who didn't make it and some who soared to heights. I firmly believe that this was due to the inability to identify what was analogue and what was digital. Below I attempt to explain those differences.

Analogue versus Digital

A main problem with some who have not embraced these changes seems to be just a general misunderstanding of what the criteria is for this Incunabula. Numerous industry experts use the terms analogue and digital: Steven Heller, Paola Antonelli and Maria Popov from the Atlantic.

Here is a quote from Steven Heller in his NY Times Sunday Book review article – *"Down to the Letters 'Graphic Design Before Graphic Designers,' and More"* - *By STEVEN HELLER OCT. 19, 2012*

> "Those who generate art, animation and even new typefaces from algorithms would not necessarily have been considered graphic designers in the analog environment, but they are becoming a new breed of designer/engineer in the digital era."

Please see other articles here on this subject.

http://www.theatlantic.com/entertainment/archive/2011/08/analog-graphic-design-to-die-for-5-fantastic-die-cut-books/244272/

http://www.nytimes.com/2012/10/21/books/review/graphic-design-before-graphic-designers-and-more.html?pagewanted=all&_r=1

http://www.moma.org/visit/calendar/exhibitions/1080

Some experts define analogue as: something that attempts to mimic the real world - a paper dummy of a product is a simple example.

Digital is defined as: something that can only exist in a digital realm.

I feel this needs to be established upfront in this book to give the reader a better platform from which to view. In all cases we need to establish if a product or service could exist realistically to the best of its desired needs in either state.

Example:

Can a website or app exist without a digital platform? – No, it can only exist via a digital platform.

Can you package and deliver consumable products virtually? – No, they are physical items and therefore can only exist in a physical state. Any prototyping of this form of packaging and delivery is merely an attempt at an analogous display.

Seems a strange point to bring up but mainly this is mentioned to establish what is or isn't analogue or digital.

Summary

Please understand this book is not meant to be a fully unabridged discussion, but rather a quick survey and reminder of how things never stay the same, but almost always are never really new. The time between them is sometimes very long, but the final effect is usually the same. As things disrupt and reform, the trick is how to absorb and use what is changing and how to use your skills to your benefit.

Chapter 3 - Winners and Losers

- Defining the sectors

"Down here it's just winners and losers. And don't get caught on the wrong side of that line"
  – Atlantic City – B. Springsteen

The disruptions are everywhere. They happen all the time. From the scribes getting the boot once movable type became popular to the workers at Disney and Kodak getting their pink slips once Jim Clarke and Steven Sasson finished their work. It is always going forward. The trick is, like a world-class surfer, how do you know which wave to ride? Like surfing, it comes with experience. So know your history – current and past.

What is the difference between disruption and innovation? Here is a strong excerpt analyzing that difference.

> *"Innovation and disruption are similar in that they are both makers and builders. Disruption takes a left turn by literally uprooting and changing how we think, behave, do business, learn and go about our day-to-day. Harvard Business School professor and disruption guru* <u>*Clayton Christensen*</u> *says that a disruption displaces an existing market, industry, or technology and produces something new and more efficient and worthwhile. It is at once destructive and creative." -* <u>*http://www.forbes.com/sites/carolinehoward/2013/03/27/you-say-innovator-i-say-disruptor-whats-the-difference/*</u>

What will affect what? And what is connected to what? Like a good programmer you must play the – if this - then that - else if – end game? The ripples affect everything in the pond. What did the Digital Incunabula disrupt? Here are just some examples that every family in America knows.

Kodak Files for Bankruptcy as Digital Era Spells End to Film

Excerpt from article is below

> *"They were a company stuck in time," said Robert Burley, an associate professor at Toronto's Ryerson University who has photographed shuttered Kodak facilities in the U.S., **Canada** and **France** since 2005. "Their history was so important to them, this rich century-old history when they made a lot of amazing things and a lot of money along the way. Now their history has become a liability."*

> *The company's credit deteriorated as revenue tumbled from traditional film, and the inventor of the Instamatic cameras was slow during the past decade to compete with Canon Inc. and Hewlett-Packard Co. in digital cameras and printers.*

> *-http://www.bloomberg.com/news/2012-01-19/kodak-photography-pioneer-files-for-bankruptcy-protection-1-.html*

And even the banking industry has felt the effects and benefits of these disruptions.

> *"Digital initiatives are also reshaping the banking industry's basic business model, a subject explored in the third article. By leveraging social and mobile capabilities, as well as cloud computing, software as a service and the advanced analytics that can help them make sense of Big Data, traditional full-service banks can drive more customer interactions at a lower unit cost. Moreover, by attracting new customer segments, the industry can develop much-needed additional sources of revenue."*

> *-   http://www.accenture.com/us-en/outlook/Pages/outlook-journal-2013-long-view-digital-disruption.aspx*

And another strong description on Digital Disruption is given in the book by the same name.

> *If people + infrastructure = disruption, then digital innovators + digital infrastructure = digital disruption. Massive digital disruption, at a scale and a pace most are simply not prepared for. Sometimes people make themselves feel better about their lack of preparation by pointing to specific failures along the way, such as the falling stock price of Facebook*

after its IPO or the inability of Groupon to figure out its business model.
http://www.huffingtonpost.com/james-mcquivey/digital-
disruption b 2868789.html

At this point I would like to break the discussion up into six sectors:

- Information
- Printing
- Promotional
- Entertainment
- Education
- The arts

Each one of these sectors has overlap, but is also unique to itself.

Information disruption

I was able to witness disruption in the information sector firsthand. While working at McGraw-Hill in 1986, I was part of the Professional and Reference Division. Our purpose was to compile and validate information needed by the professions and by the reference industry - truly my dream job. I have always read encyclopedias as a kid – nerd to the bone – albeit today a very long trip.

My job was to produce the main flagship product of the Professional and Reference Division – The Encyclopedia of Science and Technology – 6th Edition. 13,000 glorious pages of articles, figures, and diagrams. By my third year my editor-in-chief started working on putting this edition on a new media format, the CD-ROM. This was totally the domain of the programming group. I was consulted on how the screen could be designed. Not knowing a thing about designing for the screen, I quickly capitulated and stated that it was fine as it was and stepped away. But what really fascinated me was that the twenty-one volumes on the shelf now came down to two shiny discs, inclusive of text, images, and some form of audio and video. The cost to produce the printed volumes was $200US, with the cost of the compact discs being $4.95US. Compare that to the price to purchase printed volumes - $2500US. Obviously, the future was staring me in the face and unfortunately due to the shine of the disks, I was staring back.

The world of information distribution and aggregating is huge today. This is in part due to the speed and strength of the delivery of information. If you don't believe it, just look at Wall Street where information makes and breaks fortunes in a nanosecond.

Here is a quick excerpt from an interview on his new book "Flash Boys" on CBS news. Lewis explains what happens when information can be accessed faster for one investor than another.

> *"In his book "Flash Boys," author Michael Lewis explains how investors are disadvantaged without access to <u>high-frequency trade</u> technology.*
>
> *What's the advantage of speed?*
>
> *... Lewis explains how an extra millisecond allows high-frequency traders to exploit computerized trading in the U.S. stock market. By "beating" investors to exchanges, Lewis argues that high-frequency traders can buy stocks and quickly sell them back at higher prices. Billions have been spent by Wall Street firms and stock exchanges to gain the advantage of a millisecond. "Is it a scam?" 60 Minutes correspondent Steve Kroft asks. It's bigger than a scam, Lewis says. - <u>http://www.cbsnews.com/news/michael-lewis-explains-his-book-flash-boys/</u>*

What does this information have to do with the world of print? A tremendous part of the print world was dedicated to distributing financial information that brokers relied upon to make sound investments. The Financial Times was just one publication that went for $5US a daily copy over thirty years ago. Now, that information is accessed and absorbed in that nanosecond we were just talking about. Anything that takes more time is literally yesterday's news and about as valuable.

The ripples of disruption will be outlined at the end of this essay since in most cases they are similar for almost each sector.

And now this...

PA-DI – BancBoston

In reference to the disruption of the financial sector this is a personal account of what was going on during this time. One of the biggest clients we landed at Digital Interactive was BancBoston. They were the sixth largest banking system in the world and they were coming to us – a group of five people - one professor and four of his students - to create a major interactive presentation that they would use on the floor of the United States Treasury conference in Washington, D.C.

We worked on this for months including animation, video, images, and of course interactivity. We knew this was a big deal for us and we put our hearts and souls into this project. This project represented billions of dollars in revenue for BancBoston. If they had only seen our set up, a big empty warehouse with dining room chairs and a lamp extension cord running our server. A bare concrete floor, no lighting besides little desk lamps, no real salaries, no heat and barely any air-conditioning, no doors, no anything... just a desire to do great work. We finished on-time and on-budget as Larry and Rich jumped onto a little commuter prop to make the trip and show our work to the world. These kids were only 21 back then.

Printing disruption

Once the information sector had its disruptions, the printing sector would start to feel the ripples. If information in its most stoic form could be assembled and distributed in digital format, now it was time for popular culture to feel the effects. Entire magazine collections and special issues were being brought into the digital age. Images were being scanned and stored. Text was being aggregated onto these discs. The cost of printing the discs was dropping dramatically and now monthly editions of magazines were being compiled onto these discs. Encyclopedias like EST, Grolliers, and Britannica were feeling the force. Even one of the most popular magazines of the time, People, was attempting to be brought to the digital age. There were many hiccups along the way but it was clear that the plates - metaphorical tectonic ones - were shifting along with typical printing plates. Information distribution was moving and many were being left on the fading shores of that chasm.

Some of the biggest names in book printing were feeling the brunt of this new direction. Companies like R.R. Donnelly, who represented one of the largest names in printing and even down to the local printers in your neighborhood, were feeling it in lost clients and budget.

Here is an abstract detailing the health of the print industry in 1995.

"Abstract

The year 1996 should be another good one for U.S. printers and publishers. The cost pressures of 1994–95 should ease, and a stable economy with low inflation should support growth in demand for printed products. The impact of the electronic media may become further apparent in some product sectors, but a severely adverse impact on any of these sectors is unlikely. "<u>http://link.springer.com/article/10.1007/BF02680366</u>

Another article in 2009, 13 years later after the web had risen to power.

"Taking its place, of course, is the Internet, which is about to pass newspapers as a source of political news for American readers. For young people, and for the most politically engaged, it has already done so. As early as May, 2004, newspapers had become the least preferred source for news among younger people." -
<u>http://www.newyorker.com/magazine/2008/03/31/out-of-print</u>

And now today, seven years later in 2015, how is print industry faring?

"The Printing industry is in the decline stage of its life cycle. Over the 10 years to 2019, the industry's contribution to the overall economy, measured by industry value added, is expected to decline at an average annual rate of

2.6%, largely due to the increasing presence of digital media.
http://www.ibisworld.com/industry/default.aspx?indid=433

The reason to study the impact on printing is because it feels the decline in revenue from all the other sectors outlined in this book, due to the fact that it relies on those other sectors for business.

And now this...

PA-DI – Universal Interactive

Here is another personal anecdote about the print industry in its most benign form – the operating manual.

At one of the early conferences I met up with two very young executives from a company in upstate New York. The company manufactured machines that generated the components for making computers which included boards and diodes, and the physical parts that went into computers and machines that actually printed those boards. It was a huge company with plants all over a very rural campus.

They had heard me speak at a conference and thought they could use this new vehicle to better their business. The result we came up was this – instead of sending a repairperson out to the clients who bought the machines that built the boards, and in place of the manuals they printed, why not create a customer service CD-ROM?

Remember, the Web wasn't really working in 1995. So we spent the next two years building a series of CD-ROMs that could be played on the computer built into each one of the manufacturing units that Universal Instruments produced and sold.

So here was the disruption happening right at the core. The end-user was cutting out both the printer and their actual service staff by simply putting all the needed information into digital format and bundling that with each manufacturing station purchased.

The end story – one of the two gentlemen died at a very early age. The other was truly inspired and has built this knowledge base into one of the largest digital media companies in upstate New York with offices in New York City as well. His company develops interactive and video content for some of the largest players in sports, television, and other diverse forms of content.

Promotion disruption

Advertising was hit, in my opinion, the widest when these shifts happened. If the main delivery system of print was going to a digital format how could advertising keep up? CD-ROMs were one form but once the World Wide Web was launched back in 1993 all bets were off. You no longer count magazine distribution as a means to charge your ad rate; you needed to know who actually *looked* at those "pages". Not how many entire copies were being sold, but now how many pair of eyes looked at *your* ad? As with all disruptions a new industry was born where one just died. The magazine audit board was replaced by the IAB - Internet Advertising Board. New methods and processes had to be implemented. New rates and fees needed to be established. Automated processes were built – algorithms were devised – answers were required – basically, the earth shook and hasn't stopped. All of this has now grown towards becoming a powerful force in current advertising practices as traditional methodologies slowly lose dominance.

One area of "corralling" the herds back to the product from their "distraction" of being online is the constant barrage from social media platforms. To combat that distraction, brands have embraced social media and learned to properly use those benefits. Here are some excerpts from articles substantiating these effects.

Digital Ad Revenues Hit Landmark High in First Half High of 2014, Surging to $23.1 Billion, According to IAB Internet Advertising Revenue Report

Highlights of the report include:

- *Mobile revenues increased 76 percent to 5.3 billion at HY 2014, from the $3.0 billion (15% of total) reported at HY 2013, with the 2014 six month total consisting of $2.7 billion mobile search, $2.5 billion mobile display, and $103 million in other mobile formats*

- *Digital video, a component of display-related advertising, reached $1.5 billion, a 13 percent increase in revenue over the first half of 2013 at $1.3 billion*

- *Search revenues in the first half of 2014 hit $9.1 billion, up 4 percent from $8.7 billion in the first six months of 2013*

- *Display-related advertising revenues in the first half of 2014 totaled $6.5 billion, a 6 percent uptick from $6.1 billion in the first half of 2013, and accounted for 28 percent of digital advertising revenue overall*

> • *Social media revenues, which includes advertising delivered on social platforms, including social networking and social gaming websites and apps, reached $2.9 billion in HY 2014, a double-digital hike of 58 percent over the same period in 2013, at $1.9 billion*

> • *The top three advertising verticals continue to account for nearly half of advertising revenue (46%), including Retail at 21 percent, Financial Services at 13 percent and Automotive at 12 percent - See more at:* http://www.iab.net/about_the_iab/recent_press_releases/press_releas e_archive/press_release/pr-102014#sthash.Bb7ehQHa.dpuf

And how has the industry reacted to this new platform? They are investing in its future to the tune of double digits.

> *Last year, social media advertising spending was expected to reach $4.6 billion -- up 35% from $3.4 billion in 2012, according to a recent estimate from ZenithOptimedia.*

> -   *http://www.mediapost.com/publications/article/221300/brands-favor-social-media-for-local-promotions.html*

And now this...

PA-DI – TommyHilfiger,USA

As an example of disruption in the promotional sector our time with Tom-myHilfigerUSA comes to mind. Being selected by one of the biggest retailers to develop their first venture into this new digital space led us to the biggest contract we ever had during the four years of building Digital Interactive and one of our biggest names. I say *one of* because we were also getting tapped by names like American Express as well. This one contract represented over $300,000 worth of business. Through a close friend (yep – Skip DelVaglio), we were introduced to Mr. Hilfiger and we could then start work via a speculative agreement.

The one caveat – we had to work through their agency for look and feel. Well, you know the expression 'too many cooks spoil the broth'? Well, imagine *way* too many designers and especially traditional designers who knew nothing about digital. Threatened? It was like a hostage standoff. The person's name was Thatcher and it seemed he was throwing every monkey wrench into the works you could think of – again in my opinion. Because of the disconnect between print and digital mindsets, we ended up doing revision upon revision. All the while getting blamed for the 'errors'. So we started to keep a journal of these errors. I decided it should be called "Thatcher Goes A Wry".

Regardless, we finished the job to great accolades. Hilfiger wanted a touch screen display. In 1995 that didn't exist, but there was one company that was able to provide a standalone monitor that could do this with their proprietary software. Not only could you touch the screen to navigate, but you could also take a photo and store it on this computer. Nobody was doing this – anywhere – but this group of four very young geniuses were devouring these challenges step-by-step.

As a result, in over 50 MACY'S stores nationwide a kiosk of TommyHilfiger, USA would be included in that section of MACY'S. At the debut in the Herald Square store, Larry was there to make sure everything worked right. Given his instincts, he poked his head under the curtain to see if the monitor for the kiosk was working right. He noticed the screen display was set to default, a higher resolution, which made the interface screen look tiny and ridiculous. Someone possibly IT had set the resolution to the default and that made the screen image very tiny. So with Hilfiger walking down the aisle towards the kiosk surrounded by fashion press and other media Larry quickly went into the control panel reset the display, and voila the project worked.

Another quick side note – during the design phase I had mentioned that it would be cool to have a virtual dressing room since Hilfiger mainly had ensemble clothing. Every one of the 20-year olds looked at me and said, "you mean like 'Clueless'?" There was a popular movie at the time that had the main character using her computer to sort through the clothes in her wardrobe. They all laughed and said, "No way". Today, how many clothing websites have you seen that have virtual dressing rooms on them? After a while they started to really listen to me.

Entertainment disruption

Probably no sector of industry has felt the overall deep impact effect of the Digital Incunabula like the entertainment industry. From the earliest days of Todd Rundgren building his own digital studio and releasing his albums to Sean Parker peeking into your hard drive at home, the entertainment industry - especially the music industry - quickly became the first casualty of this new age. No longer do record stores line the strip malls or the avenues. No longer must you save up for a $20 album; now you can just buy the one song. No longer do you have to fork over $100 to bring the family to the movies; now you swipe up the movie using services like ChromeCast from your tablet to your big screen television - all for $7.99 a month. Movies have started to price themselves out of the family market and it has become a serpent eating its own tail effect. The days of the huge summer blockbuster are fast becoming memories. Now music industry standards for a gold album have dropped to numbers in the 100,000 as opposed to the 1,000,000 mark.

> *"Since the introduction of the iTunes Music Store on April 28, 2003, music sales have plummeted in the United States -- from $11.8 billion in 2003 to $7.1 billion last year, according to the Recording Industry Association of America." -* [*http://money.cnn.com/2013/04/25/technology/itunes-music-decline/*](http://money.cnn.com/2013/04/25/technology/itunes-music-decline/)

The movie industry has also felt the brunt of these disruptions from increases in digital piracy to hacks on computer systems, and a drop in summer blockbuster revenue.

> *"Large declines aren't uncommon in the blockbuster business, where so much of the marketing push is for opening weekend. But such steep fall-offs contribute to anxiety over the ability of movies to capture and hold the attention of moviegoers in an age of so many other entertainment options."* –[*http://www.pressherald.com/2014/07/10/with-few-blockbusters-hollywoods-summer-box-office-revenues-drop/*](http://www.pressherald.com/2014/07/10/with-few-blockbusters-hollywoods-summer-box-office-revenues-drop/)

> *"Between the first weekend in May through the end of August, ticket sales in the United States and Canada are expected to total roughly $3.9 billion, a 15 percent decline from the same stretch last year, according to Rentrak, a box office data company."-* [*http://www.nytimes.com/2014/08/30/movies/movies-have-worst-summer-since-1997.html?_r=0*](http://www.nytimes.com/2014/08/30/movies/movies-have-worst-summer-since-1997.html?_r=0)

How will this ripple back through the overall economic landscape. Well, think for a second about how many people are employed by the entertainment industry and how those same people will be looking for new jobs. The same goes for other areas in the entertainment field.

Read an excerpt from Home Media Magazine detailing a bit of the disruptions felt in the entertainment field.

> *"As has long been noted, the revenue model that has underpinned the entire Hollywood ecosystem is under assault. The theatrical business looks shaky. The summer box office disappointed, as consumers found other things to do (including watching digital content)..." -*
> *http://www.homemediamagazine.com/steph-sums-it/4-types-digital-disruption*

How has television been affected by this new Digital Incunabula? The first answer is greatly. The television industry has been fractured in the last ten years, from the effects of YouTube to Hulu to now - how every website out there is embedding video into almost every story and byline. How have they dealt with it? Many excerpts that follow will explain.

When Edison first started the motion picture industry his original studio the Black Mariah was basically a hallway of dozens of small rooms all in a line. A camera, operator and a director on one side with the scene and actors in front of them, with each of the scenes and actors dressed in storyline and acting. Each small vignette was captured on film and then distributed via the Nickelodeon or to simple movie houses.

Now that model is being replicated over a hundred years later by companies like HuffingtonPost, msnbc, NBC, ABC, CBS, and every one of the major networks and news organizations. These small setups capture the content and distribute it out via today's Nickelodeon – the Internet – to homes and individuals around the world.

You would think anything interactive-based would be untouchable, but see this article concerning of all companies - Disney.

> *"The Mouse House's lone lame-duck operation Disney Interactive has made entertainment financial wags' predictions come true by enacting an estimated 700 layoffs, or 26% of its workforce. As Deadline's financial editor notes, DI (Disney Interactive) was the company's only money-losing division in the fiscal year which ended last September. Along with staff cuts, DI [Disney Interactive] will be halving the number of games it puts out yearly and will reduce the number of concepts it develops in-house in order to make room for outside licenses. It will also shut down websites BabyZone and Spoonful while looking for more online advertising support for Disney.com.*
>
> *- http://www.animationmagazine.net/top-stories/disney-interactive-slashes-700-jobs/*

So nothing is exempt or sacred, not even the platform, which created this beast. Take into account all of the different avenues to get your entertainment - whether music, movies, games, books, etc. All the major networks are now putting the content online and some for free. Notice how the music industry has felt the blow year after year.

Here is just a short list of the dedicated platforms and devices from which consumers can stream their desired content anytime, anywhere.

- Amazon Prime
- Hulu
- iPad
- iPhone
- iTunes
- Kindle
- LiveGame
- Netflix
- Nook
- Pandora
- Spotify
- Youtube

And now this...

PA-DI – ITV NYNEX/Verizon

One of the main duties as a consultant for this company was for me to travel the country giving speeches and conferences on this new media. And as luck would have it after a Boston trip we received an RFP (Request for Proposal) from NYNEX (now Verizon).

They wanted us to develop an interface prototype for their new Interactive Television service. I mention Boston because low and behold the service would debut in Boston. So they send the RFP and I did a quick write up. I spec'd the time and costs and what we would provide. They were so taken by it that we got the go-ahead right away, and the team started to work on what it would look and operate like.

Again, I had to go away for another conference and when I returned, the team – Janice, Larry, Joe and Rich – all wanted me to see what they had built. This is where the true genius of this team comes into focus. Using everything they had learned to date they had built a scrollable image menu that was segregated into the different interests a user would have – movies, events, clothing, dining, tourism, etc. all mouse-controlled.

Little did we know Jim Clarke of Netscape and Silicon Graphics fame was working with NYNEX on the other end of the project in Orlando, Florida – the Orlando Project? So here we are in a warehouse out on Long Island working literally and figuratively in the dark with one of the biggest Internet Service Providers in the world and almost against one of the pioneers of the World Wide Web.

X-Ice

We did some work for a little sports team you might have heard of... the NHL's NY Islanders. Our team, through Joe's connection, won the bid to build their first website, which they wanted to call it X-Ice. We built a hockey game on the website where you could actually play and score goals. It was very similar to a dressed up Pong, but it won one of the first Shockwave Gallery awards that was ever given out. Later, we had a shot at the revised version – and we were off. We shoot - we score!

Education disruption

From the first incunabulum to today the world of education hasn't actually changed much. Students are still taught in a rote manner – memorization is still the key to learning. Although there have been many attempts to change the model, it is basically the same since the late 1800's at best. From law school to medical school to the study of education itself, memorization is still a large part of the process. In my opinion, these schools are vocational – if not, I hope so. I hope my lawyer and my doctor know their vocation. Basically, the professions have always held a place as not "vocational" but some space in between a Ph.D. and a M.D. or J.D.? A never, never land where even in academia only recently have such degrees like a J.D. (Juris Doctorate) been seen as a terminal degree. But never the less such degrees do represent finality to that area of study, and they are again vocational.

To me, it appears that the pendulum has swung again from pure theory to application, and is now settling in the middle to provide a balance of both: applied theory. Many have attempted to change this model as individual universities, school districts, and teachers, but it would seem the biggest change might have to come from the bottom up; through the desire to use and the direct response by students to these new learning techniques, aids, and requirements.

The growth of online education has been staggering in the last five years alone.

Key report findings include:

- *Over 6.7 million students were taking at least one online course during the fall 2011 term, an increase of 570,000 students over the previous year*

- *Thirty-two percent of higher education students now take at least one course online*

- *Only 2.6 percent of higher education institutions currently have a MOOC (Massive Open Online Course), another 9.4 percent report MOOCs are in the planning stages*

- *Academic leaders remain unconvinced that MOOCs represent a sustainable method for offering online courses, but do believe that they provide an important means for institutions to learn about online pedagogy*

- *Seventy-seven percent of academic leaders rate the learning outcomes in online education as the same or superior to those in face-to-face*

- *Only 30.2 percent of chief academic officers believe that their faculty accept the value and legitimacy of online education - a rate is lower than recorded in 2004*

- *The proportion of chief academic leaders that say that online learning is critical to their long-term strategy is at a new high of 69.1 percent*

- *A majority of chief academic officers at all types of institutions continue to believe that lower retention rates for online courses are a barrier to the wide-spread adoption of online education.* –

http://onlinelearningconsortium.org/survey report/changing-course-ten-years-tracking-online-education-united-states/

How far has it come from 2006? See excerpt from same source detailing up to that time period.

How Many Students are Learning Online?

Background: *For the past several years, online enrollments have been growing substantially faster than overall higher education enrollments. The expectation of academic leaders has been that these enrollments would continue their substantial growth for at least another year. Do the measured enrollments match these lofty expectations?*

The evidence: *Online enrollments have continued to grow at rates far in excess of the total higher education student population, albeit at slower rates than for previous years.*

- *Almost 3.5 million students were taking at least one online course during the fall 2006 term; a nearly 10 percent increase over the number reported the previous year*

- *The 9.7 percent growth rate for online enrollments far exceeds the 1.5 percent growth of the overall higher education student population*

- *Nearly twenty percent of all U.S. higher education students were taking at least one online course in the fall of 2006*

What are the Prospects for Future Online Enrollment Growth?

Background: *Compound annual enrollment growth rates of over twenty percent are not sustainable. The demand for online among potential students is finite, as is the ability of institutions to grow existing offerings or add new ones. Where can we expect the additional growth to occur?*
The evidence: *Approximately one-third of higher education institutions account for three-quarters of all online enrolments. Future growth will come predominately from these and similar institutions as they add new programs and grow existing ones.*

- *Much of the past growth in online enrollments has been fueled by new institutions entering the online learning arena. This transition is now nearing its end; most institutions that plan to offer online education are already doing so.*

- *A large majority (69 percent) of academic leaders believe that student demand for online learning is still growing*

- *Virtually all (83 percent) institutions with online offerings expect their online enrollments to increase over the coming year*

- *Future growth in online enrollments will most likely come from those institutions that are currently the most engaged; they enroll the most online learning students and have the highest expectations for growth*

- http://olc.onlinelearningconsortium.org/publications/survey/online_nation

In contrast, but only minimally given that almost no one is advocating fully online curriculum and courseware, blended learning allows students to be moderated and guided by - of course a teacher; see the article below. Specifically note that this is speaking to a "fully online" process.

Effectiveness of Fully Online Courses for College Students: Response to a Department of Education Meta-Analysis

Jaggars, Shanna Smith; Bailey, Thomas

Community College Research Center, Columbia University

Proponents of postsecondary online education were recently buoyed by a meta-analysis sponsored by the U.S. Department of Education suggesting that, in many cases, student learning outcomes in online courses are superior to those in traditional face-to-face courses. This finding does not hold, however, for the studies included in the meta-analysis that pertain to fully online, semester-length college courses; among these studies, there is no trend in favor of the online course mode. What is more, these studies consider courses that were taken by relatively well-prepared university students, so their results may not generalize to traditionally underserved populations. Therefore, while advocates argue that online learning is a promising means to increase access to college and to improve student progression through higher education programs, the Department of Education report does not present evidence that fully online delivery produces superior learning outcomes for typical college courses, particularly among low-income and academically underprepared students. - http://eric.ed.gov/?id=ED512274

I am sure I don't need to explain how the growth of online education changes the field of publishing and print.

Sales of new printed textbooks made up 38% of McGraw-Hill Education's higher-ed revenue in 2013, down from 71% in 2010, said Chief Executive and President David Levin.

Meanwhile, sales of cheaper "customized" books—individual chapters modified by professors for a particular course—are rising at a double-digit percentage. So are computer-software programs, which are generally cheaper than print textbooks. They offer the contents of textbooks and track students' progress with quizzes, Mr. Levin said.- http://www.wsj.com/articles/a-tough-lesson-for-college-textbook-publishers-1409182139

Here again is more from David Levin on the subject via a August 2015 article on HuffingtonPost.com – mentioned before in this book.

"The value proposition of digital learning *Digital is not without its own costs. Devices and software require invest-ment; so does bandwidth, IT support and training. "Uptime" isn't a concern when an instructor adopts a textbook. But even with these expenses, the right technology can make a very real difference in lowering the long-term cost of education.*

Studies have shown that students using technologies designed to personalize the learning experience get better grades and have greater success completing their courses. And for the 50% of two-year college students and 20% of four-year college students taking remedial courses, these technologies can help them catch up with their peers and get back on track to an on-time degree. When you factor in the cost of tuition and increased earning potential of college graduates, it becomes clear that these outcomes can change lives.

To put the value in real terms, consider a biology textbook of ours that costs around $190 at the college bookstore. We now offer a better option--a digital, personalized version for $85. The digital version is more than just an e-book: it focuses stu-dents' attention on the concepts they need to learn most and away from what they've already learned. It's been shown to help students get a better grade. Stacking these options side by side, it becomes clear that digital is simply a better value than print. We feel so strongly about this point that we now offer college students who buy our digital products the option to add a loose-leaf print version for what's essentially a pro-cessing fee--only $15 for most college courses."

http://www.huffingtonpost.com/david-levin/dear-students-and-faculty_b_7957508.html

Some other areas of concern and innovation are listed below and will be discussed later in the chapter "The Real Ripples".

- Common Core
- Tablets in the classroom
- Use of the Internet as a learning tool
- eTextbooks
- Gen-I
- STEM & STEAM
- MOOCs

And now this...

<u>PA-DI – Icons: Thesis work</u>

The evolution of online education has always been of interest to me and during the time of my work in achieving my Masters' degree I developed an interactive CD-ROM like I had witnessed at McGraw-Hill.

Concurrent with teaching a full load, consulting with Digital Interactive, being a freelance art director at a friend's company, doing a major renovation to the house, trying to raise two young children, and helping a terminally ill parent, I was also going for my Masters degree. And we were also then - and still are - a one income household.

I started my Masters in 1990 and had been going part time during summers, and sometimes during the school year. Now it was time for my thesis project. I had been focusing on (of course) multimedia and specifically the use of multimedia in higher education. I had learned a lot, not from the courses, but from doing it. So I sat down to build my thesis project. I had been compiling all of the content needed, text, images, audio, and video. It was called Icons. I had focused on Art History - specifically the Dada movement because it was so multimedia in its nature. I chose to focus on Marcel Duchamp because of his diversity in image, film, audio, painting, and writing, just a wide range of work. To this end I built a CD-ROM that allowed the user to cycle through his work and to see other artists' work from the same period along with current affairs and historical footage. You even had the ability to take notes and tests within the program.

Building this took three weeks during the summer, with all of the things I described happening around me. My kids were 7 and 4, and were scurrying around my feet while I tried to program this project. Now in the middle of this I received a letter from the school I was teaching at telling me I was denied tenure because I didn't finish my degree in the allotted time frame. A *truly dear* colleague lied to administration about my progress. So with all of these things going on, I now had to sue them. I won - four people had to take early retirement - but it wreaked havoc on my family to this day. Oh and by the way – both my mother and father died in the midst of all of this just 78 days apart.

Somehow or another I finished it all up. I presented a finished 191 page written thesis and authored an interactive CD-ROM. I received my degree and won in New York State Supreme Court. - http://caselaw.findlaw.com/ny-supreme-court/1170198.html

One of my colleagues and some of my students who used the prototype remarked that they wouldn't want to learn or teach Art History any other way. I was approached by Pearson to bring it to market. Obviously with all that was going on, that one fell by the wayside. It was a big regret, but there was only so much of me to go around back then.

Arts disruption

For over 50 years the arts have felt the effect of the computer. From the days of Billy Kluver and E.A.T. the arts have dabbled in the use of technology to create art. In 2002, that erupted at the Whitney Biennale. Artists like Mark Napier, Lisa Jevbratt, John Maeda, Margot Lovejoy, Future Farmers, Benjamin Fry, broke open the use of digital space and the entrance of code as an art form. Sure, artists had used computers to create video or printed computer graphics but now the user became part of the artwork and it only existed in a conceptual ephemeral space. The problem that seemed to cut at the base was – 'could you actually sell the work?' Here is where a large discussion on value came into play. Conceptual thinking such as, 'did the art actually exist without the user?' The prospect of value challenged the existence of the work. They tried virtual galleries but it wasn't the same, in my opinion, even in the remotest possibility. It was like trying to shove one aesthetic into the other. If art was supposed to be for the masses then how could the art world refute this attempt and manor of global distribution? And if the goal was to communicate the experience, how could a user being a necessary component challenge and invalidate the method? It was a huge shift, and of course thirteen years later nothing has really come of it. Just like the economic models of many industries it will have to be simply beaten into submission by lack of dollars in the traditional marketplace or a massive devaluing of the commodity. This is what I believe is happening right now.

As examples of those economic influences just think back to the news on Kodak's bankruptcy. Now apply that to the study of photography. Due to these breakthroughs in technology everybody thinks they can be a decent photographer – and to some point, they can. SO what has that done to the area of major like pure Art Photography?

To see how hard it was for the world of interactive art to break through here is a review of the Whitney Biennale 2002 by Carter B. Horsley in The City Review and Holland Cotter from the New York Times.

Please note that this show heralded the world of interactive art and showcased the interactive art of some who now have completely changed the landscape. Even as recent as 13 years ago it seems reviewers had no idea what was going on. The show had 113 artists and was over 85% digital. The excerpts below were all I could find on the Internet that even referenced, these interactive and digital work

Whitney Biennale 2002

By Carter B. Horsley

> *If the Whitney Biennial is a good reflection of what is exceptional in contemporary art, then the state of contemporary art in 2002 is pretty sad as*

the vast majority of works exhibited this year are puerile and without much merit.

The biggest show in two decades, this biennial highlights the works of 113 artists in a variety of media and there is more architecture, performance, Internet and "sound art" in this biennial than ever before. If the overall verdict for the biennial is disappointment and ennui at what mostly is a ghastly mess, a few works, nonetheless, are outstanding and memorable. - http://www.thecityreview.com/biennial.html

ART REVIEW; Spiritual America, From Ecstatic To Transcendent By HOLLAND COTTER

Published: March 8, 2002

YESTERDAY was the opening of the 2002 Whitney Biennial, the show that's supposed to take the pulse of contemporary American art and that almost always gets the art world's knickers in a twist. Score-settlers and list fetishists have fits. Last time around, a lot of people were just dismissive. American art is out of steam, the idea was, and here's the proof.

... The Internet is the ultimate (so far, anyway) tribal site, with all the implications of concord and conflict that implies. And the biennial's program of Internet- and software-based art, organized by the adjunct curator of new media arts, Christiane Paul, approaches it that way.

A Web site by Margot Lovejoy is a repository for accounts of changed lives (www.myturningpoint.com). Another, by Mark Napier, tests the Internet's border-breaching unruliness (www.potatoland.org /riot). A third, by Josh On and Futurefarmers, zeroes in on the politics of electronic communication, tracking the usually hidden links among the corporations that have commandeered digital media as a marketing tool (www.theyrule.net). - http://www.nytimes.com/2002/03/08/arts/art-review-spiritual-america-from-ecstatic-to-transcendent.html

Now here is a short list of some of the interactive artists and who they have become.

Benjamin Fry

Ben Fry is principal of Fathom, a design and software consultancy located in Boston. He received his doctoral degree from the Aesthetics + Computation Group at the MIT Media Laboratory, where his research focused on combining fields such as computer science, statistics, graphic design, and data visualization as a means for understanding information.

http://benfry.com/about/

Lisa Jevbratt

b 1967 in Vaxholm (S); lives in San José (USA).

Lisa Jevbratt is a Swedish research theorist, systems and Internet artist. Her projects explore data mining, organizational structures, information filtering, data organization and mapping, aesthetic, political, and cultural implications of the languages and protocols of emerging technologies.

- http://www.medienkunstnetz.de/artist/jevbratt/biography/

Margot Lovejoy

Margot Lovejoy is Professor of Visual Arts at the State University of New York at Purchase and author of \ \ \ "Postmodern Currents: Art and Artists in the Age of Electronic Media\ \ \ " (1997). She is recipient of a 1988 Guggenheim Fellowship and a 1994 Arts International Grant in India. Exhibited internationally, she has had many solo exhibitions in and around New York including those at the Alternative Museum; P.S.#1 Contemporary Art Center; Newhouse Center for Contemporary Art; Queens Museum of Art; Neuberger Museum of Art; Stamford Museum and the Islip Museum. - http://rhizome.org/profiles/margotlovejoy/

John Maeda

John Maeda is Partner at Kleiner Perkins Caufield & Byers, and also Chair of the eBay Inc Design Advisory Board. He actively bridges technology, design, and leadership. His work as an artist, graphic designer, computer scientist and educator earned him the distinction of being named one of the 75 most influential people of the 21st century by Esquire. As a professor at the MIT Media Lab starting in 1996, Maeda led research that brought together technologists, designers, and business leaders into a common space of possibility. Maeda's early work -- bridging advanced computation with traditional visual art -- is represented in the permanent collection of the Museum of Modern Art. http://about.me/johnmaeda

Mark Napier

Mark Napier, a painter turned digital artist, packed up his paints in 1995 to create artwork exclusively for the Web. Since then he has produced a wide range of Internet projects including The Shredder, an alternative browser that dematerializes the web, Digital Landfill, an endless archive of digital debris, and ©Bots, a tool for building unique pop-culture icons from parts.   -
http://www.sfmoma.org/exhib_events/exhibitions/details/espace_napier#ixzz3OVtUnd9s

And now here are two of my favorites in the world of Data Visualization and truly interactive art. Why? Because they do the actual work not a fake version of it.

Tim Otto Roth

Tim Otto Roth was born in 1974 in Oppenau in the Black Forest. 1994-1995 he studied politics and philosophy in Tübingen (Germany) and moved in 1995 to study fine arts at the University of Kassel (D). After graduation 2001 he was appointed master student at Floris M. Neusüss. 2004 followed by a second degree in the theory of visual communication. In the winter of 2014 he successfully defended his dissertation at the Academy of Media Arts in Cologne. He lives and works in Oppenau and Cologne.

- http://www.imachination.net/about.html

Camille Utterback - Ms. Utterback is also a MacArthur Award winner.

Camille Utterback is a pioneering digital artist whose interactive installations and reactive sculptures engage participants in a dynamic process of kinesthetic discovery and play. Utterback's work explores the aesthetic and experiential possibilities of linking computational systems to human movement and gesture in layered and often humorous ways. Her work focuses attention on the continued relevance and richness of the body in our increasingly mediated world.

- *http://atc.berkeley.edu/bio/Camille_Utterback/*

I know, I know art is in the eye of the beholder. But how could a group like this be so overlooked? My answer – the byproduct could not be packaged and sold like traditional forms of art. So therefore it couldn't or wouldn't be substantiated or promoted. Something so relevant and not that far ahead of its time was just left to kind of die off?

Well think about Walter Benjamin and his 1936 essay "The Work of Art in the Age of Mechanical Reproduction". I use this essay in class. Benjamin's main point seems to be that there is an "aura" around a singular piece of art that any form of reproduction can never capture.

"One might subsume the eliminated element in the term "aura" and go on to say: that which withers in the age of mechanical reproduction is the aura of the work of art." -
https://www.marxists.org/reference/subject/philosophy/works/ge/benjamin.htm

While that's a great argument, it just labels the art as a commodity – one of wealth, whether it is a cultural commodity or an actual commodity. After all, I guess it's all about the "Benjamins" – the real paper "Benjamins". But should this be true even when we deal with something as supposedly pure and clean as art?

And now this...

PA-DI – GoldSchlager

At Digital Interactive we got the chance to work with one of the smaller agencies in Manhattan but they had a great account and they wanted a very interesting product developed. Since back then there really wasn't much call for interactive art, the closest we got to that kind of work was an interactive screen saver for an ad agency that handled a liquor named Goldschlager.

The uniqueness of the product at the time was that it had actual flakes of gold floating in the liquor. You used it for shots, and I guess it was a big deal. So we got the work from a NYC agency, but here was the catch - they wanted it in a 3D mode. You know the kind where you had to wear the red and green glasses to see it.

Larry – the head designer and developer got to work. He learned how to actually create the stereoscopic image and how to program the two images to follow each other around the screen close enough so that when you wore the glasses it looked like a 3 dimensional image. It actually worked when the computer went into sleep mode, and for all intents and purposes it was exactly what they client wanted.

So now what was a major business could be easily replicated on a simple computer running $300 software - major disruptor.

But think of how this could be applied to interactive art - image, motion, interactivity, audio, and video – really a blank open canvas.

Chapter 4 - The ripple effect

How big and how far do these ripples reach? Well just think about it. Craigslist destroyed the newspaper industry as we knew it. It killed the main revenue stream by allowing classified ads to be placed online for free. Classified ads were over 50% of the newspaper industries revenue. Even a field that was once seen as very stable, like the educational publishing industry, has seen these disruptions. These changes have sent that entire business model and the rest of them; information, publishing, promotion, entertainment, education, and the arts into a tailspin from which they still haven't recovered or reinvented themselves. Many individuals have had to re-invent themselves numerous times, as have their respective fields, due to these new digital changes and shifts.

In this chapter I want to give examples of these ripple effects on each sector, but try to show how they are all interrelated.

Starting with education (because that is where it all starts) this excerpt shows how the education sector has suffered major shifts as well.

"Rising costs could scarcely strike at a worse time. Around the world demand for retraining and continuing education is soaring among workers of all ages. Globalisation and automation have shrunk the number of jobs requiring a middling level of education. Those workers with the means to do so have sought more education, in an attempt to stay ahead of the labour-demand curve. In America, higher-education enrolment by students aged 35 or older rose by 314,000 in the 1990s, but by 899,000 in the 2000s." –

http://www.economist.com/news/briefing/21605899-staid-higher-education-business-about-experience-welcome-earthquake-digital

Now this is where the serpent starts eating its tail – in its education demands.

"... the Internet has created a demand for digital textbooks, which has reduced the revenue of the established publishers. In the higher education market — primarily a B2C market where textbooks are sold to individual students — the price a publisher can command for a digital version of a textbook is lower than that of a physical copy. In the K-12 market — primarily a B2B market where textbooks are sold to school districts — publishers typically charge a school district an annual subscription fee for an e-textbook, which defers income. For example, a publisher could sell a physical textbook for $75, but could only charge $12.50 for an annual subscription fee for the ebook version of that textbook. While over six years the revenue stream would total $75, in the first year the publisher's revenue is down $62.50."

"Probably even more transformational is the Open Educational Resources (OERs) approach. OERs are released under an open license that permits their free use and repurposing." –

http://www.project-disco.org/competition/112113-the-changing-textbook-industry/

The entertainment industry has also felt the effect of this directly on the sales of product. Even such veterans and music icons like David Bowie saw how this would impact the future of the overall entertainment industry.

"I don't even know why I would want to be on a label in a few years, because I don't think it's going to work by labels and by distribution systems in the same way. The absolute transformation of everything that we ever thought about music will take place within 10 years, and nothing is going to be able to stop it"- David Bowie (excerpt from the 2002 New York Times article "David Bowie, 21st Century Entrepreneur" by Jon Pareles)

The transference of those skills and shift and shrinking of jobs, from the disruption is explained here.

"The increase, of 0.3 percent, was tiny, and the total revenue, $16.5 billion, was a far cry from the $38 billion that the industry took in at its peak more than a decade ago. Still, even if it is not time for the record companies to party like it's 1999, the figures, reported Tuesday by the International Federation of the Phonographic Industry, provide significant encouragement."

"Now music executives, having been written off as dinosaurs, are finding their skills and knowledge back in demand.

Book publishers in London and New York, for example, have been hiring digital experts away from record companies, analysts say, as they seek to build up their e-book businesses.

Had the music industry been more open to change in 1999, some analysts say they believe, it might not have taken more than a decade to get to this stage.

"If there is a lesson to take away, it is probably that the earlier you can embrace new business models and services, the better," said Paul Brindley, chief executive of Music Ally, a consulting firm in London. "Whether this is signaling a turnaround that will lead to inexorable growth, who knows? But it does at least signal a bottoming out, with room for growth."

- http://www.nytimes.com/2013/02/27/technology/music-industry-records-first-revenue-increase-since-1999.html?_r=0

And these same disruptions are just as prevalent in the newspaper and magazine industry, with less of a lack of crossing over the existing skill sets.

"THE AMERICAN NEWSPAPER MEDIA INDUSTRY REVENUE PROFILE 2012

Overall, total revenue for U.S. newspapers declined by 2% in 2012 from a year earlier, according to new data compiled by the Newspaper Association of America.

In total, the U.S. newspaper media industry took in $38.6 billion in 2012 compared with $39.5 billion in revenue in 2011, according to NAA's projections.

The numbers reveal that while advertising revenue continues to decline— down 6% in 2012—several other categories of newspaper media revenue are now growing. Circulation revenue grew 5% in 2012, while a host of new revenue sources not tied to conventional advertising and that barely existed a few years ago grew by 8%. These new revenue sources, which include such items as digital consulting for local business and e-commerce transactions, now account for close to one-in-ten dollars coming into newspaper media companies. They are significant enough in scale that NAA has begun to collect detailed data about these revenue categories and track their trajectory year-to-year for the first time." –

http://www.naa.org/trends-and-numbers/newspaper-revenue/newspaper-media-industry-revenue-profile-2012.aspx

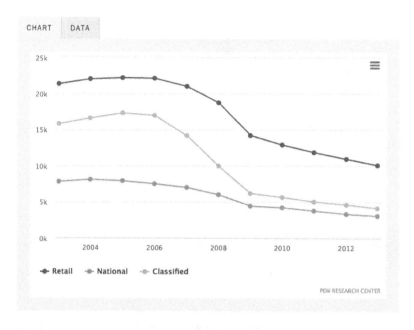

In Millions of Dollars

Note: 2013 data were updated based on percentage changes from 2012. Both retail and national advertising declined 8% and classified advertising declined 10.5%.

Source: Newspaper Association of America

http://www.journalism.org/media-indicators/newspaper-revenue-from-retail-national-and-classified-ads/

Magazines also found the loss of revenue from classifieds rolled downstream and upstream to cause disruption in the traditional ad revenue model. Agencies had to adapt to a new model as well. No longer could they bill a direct 15% for ad placement; now the ads had to actually work for them to get that commission. The old adage of "I know half of my advertising doesn't work, I just don't know which half" wasn't true anymore. Now analytics could tell you which half wasn't working and now clients weren't willing to pay for that half. Companies like DoubleClick were making the rules. Soon acquired by Google, the monster in the box was going to come out and drive the bus.

Today a good portion of the advertising media buys are built on an auction structure. As news trends or celebrity stories spike the ad space on that site spikes as well. Now an entire monthly ad buy budget could be wiped out based on one big trending story.

Magazine Revenue Remains Flat in 2010

Percent Change in Ad Pages Sold

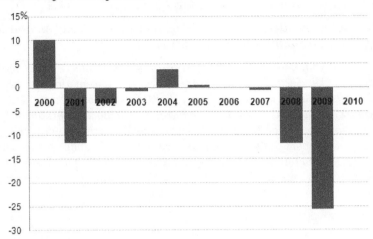

Source: Publishers Information Bureau, of the Association of Magazine Media
PEW RESEARCH CENTER'S PROJECT FOR EXCELLENCE IN JOURNALISM
2011 STATE OF THE NEWS MEDIA

http://www.stateofthemedia.org/2011/magazines-essay/data-page-4/

Book publishing has seen a straight decline in traditional book sales for the last 5 years. E-books are quickly outselling traditional print in both consumer and college sales.
http://www.nytimes.com/2011/05/20/technology/20amazon.html?_r=0

But what does this mean as far as an economic model, how does it affect society at large? Quick statistic from Forbes – needed employees for Amazon versus traditional retailers -

14 - The number of workers Amazon employs for every $10 million in revenue it generates. For brick-and-mortar retailers, the average is 47 employees per $10 million of revenue.

http://www.forbes.com/sites/jeffbercovici/2014/02/10/amazon-vs-book-publishers-by-the-numbers/

So now that these effects are becoming more and more a part of our everyday lives, what does actually affect individuals? And how can those individuals and the educational system that hopes to prepare them properly evolve? What can be done?

At M.I.T. there are studies to evaluate this – a short excerpt is below:

Erik Brynjolfsson – Deep Understanding, Improvement, and Measurement of Labor, Wage Inequality, and Economic Health

In his recent book with IDE co-director Andrew McAfee, Erik Brynjolfsson explores The Second Machine Age—*a core concept in his research. Brynjolfsson looks at the increasing digitization of our society and, while acknowledging and celebrating the dramatic impact on productivity and the many fascinating things we have been able to achieve with technology, studies its impact on labor and jobs. "We're trying to understand how technology is changing the workforce," he says. "Technology has rushed ahead, but there are implications in terms of social impact and the need for managers and educators to adjust, and those changes are slower."*

http://mitsloan.mit.edu/ide/research/

In one recent project, Brynjolfsson and his team have undertaken a systematic analysis of all the occupations in the United States, examined the capabilities required for each job, and determined which skills are being automated and which are in increasing demand. The findings could help shape educational policy and workforce training efforts. "We have an educational system designed for a 20th century economy," says Brynjolfsson, with students trained to memorize and follow instructions and rules, an approach initially designed to prepare them for factory work that today is largely mechanized. Instead, Brynjolfsson argues for an emphasis on creative thinking and problem-solving skills that will enable students to go on to the sorts of jobs that can only be done by humans – and tend to offer higher financial and emotional rewards as well. - http://mitsloan.mit.edu/ide/research/

Brynjolfsson doesn't propose to have all the answers but he certainly lays out a road map and path to make this needed transformation happen. He, with other experts, have spoken directly about their respective fields and how they intertwine and affect each other. This next section presents some of the experts in these fields and their viewpoints on the future of those respective areas of study.

Chapter 5 - The ripple experts

Defining design in the 21st century

In my humble opinion design is quickly becoming the hallmark of the 21st century. In a discussion with colleagues I stated that I believe that "the 19th century was arts and crafts, the 20th century was art, and now the 21st century is all about design."

Why focus on design? Remember Antonelli's answer (and more from her later).

> "In truth, design has spread like gas to almost all facets of human activity, from science and education to politics and policymaking. For a simple reason: one of design's most fundamental tasks is to help people deal with change."

Again in my opinion as well, design is no longer just an ornamentation to be used to persuade. Now it is integrated into how we interact with products. Now that so much of our experiences are in a digital format the main experience has left the hand and moved directly to the brain. The content and the delivery method have become one. Like any other symbiotic relationship one tremendously influences the other. Design is no longer about the curtains or the difference between khaki and beige. Now it is at the forefront of the experience. It is making the experience work or not. Later we will speak about Interaction Design.

It is my belief that this is due to the disruption caused by the Digital Incunabula. As discussed before jobs, products, services have had to become more efficient due to a slow down in economic resources. Those slowdowns are due to the changes caused by going to a digital age. From paper to pixels, as we have said for years.

So how does this all play out and where should we put our efforts? Well, that's where my validity ends. I do not propose to say that I am in any way a definitive source for this discussion, so I turned to truly respected sources – Nicholas Negroponte, Sir Ken Robinson, Paola Antonelli, John Maeda, and David Kelley. Many of these areas overlap – for instance the approach to design and the teaching of design overlap all areas – information, publishing, promotion, entertainment, education, and the arts.

Listed below are short bios for these individuals and some information regarding their beliefs on the needed steps to improve the design of their respective sectors.

Nicholas Negroponte

Nicholas Negroponte is founder and chairman of the One Laptop per Child non-profit association. He was co-founder and director of the MIT Media Lab, and the Jerome B. Wiesner Professor of Media Technology. A graduate of MIT, Negroponte was a pioneer in the field of computer-aided design, and has been a member of the MIT faculty since 1966. Conceived in 1980, the Media Lab opened its doors in 1985. He is also author of the 1995 best seller, Being Digital, which has been translated into more than 40 languages. In the private sector, Negroponte serves on the board of directors for Motorola, Inc. and as general partner in a venture capital firm specializing in digital technologies for information and entertainment. He has provided start-up funds for more than 40 companies, including Wired magazine. - http://www.media.mit.edu/people/nicholas

Negroponte's book "Being Digital" in 1995 confirmed every belief I had in what was happening then and what would happen later. In 1994, before I knew of Negroponte, I was consulting for that start up digital agency. I tried to get the investors to understand what I was advocating. I hired some people who I thought would get the vision. In time "Being Digital" got published. I gave my copy to the main sales person. He looked at me and said, "this is everything you have been talking about!" the difference – I wasn't Negroponte.

I often ask my classes if their concepts for thesis projects were "bits or atoms"? His story of the value of data over physical inventory basically heralded the economic models of today here is an excerpt on that discussion.

"I recently visited the headquarters of one of the United States' top five integrated-circuit manufacturers. I was asked to sign in and, in the process, was asked whether I had a laptop computer with me. Of course I did. The receptionist asked for the model, serial number, and the computer's value. "Roughly US$1 to $2 million," I said. "Oh, that cannot be, sir," she replied. "What do you mean? Let me see it."

I showed her my old PowerBook (whose PowerPlate makes it an impressive 4 inches thick), and she estimated its value at $2,000. She wrote down that amount and I was allowed to enter." -
http://web.media.mit.edu/~nicholas/Wired/WIRED3-01.html

Beyond Digital

Sometimes defining the spirit of an age can be as simple as a single word. You may remember, for instance, the succinct (if somewhat cryptic) career advice given to young Benjamin Braddock, played by Dustin Hoffman, in the 1967 film The Graduate: "Plastics."

"Exactly how do you mean?" asked Ben.

"There's a great future in plastics," replied Mr. McGuire. "Think about it. Will you think about it?"

Now that we're in that future, of course, plastics are no big deal. Is digital destined for the same banality? Certainly. Its literal form, the technology, is already beginning to be taken for granted, and its connotation will become tomorrow's commercial and cultural compost for new ideas. Like air and drinking water, being digital will be noticed only by its absence, not its presence."
- http://archive.wired.com/wired/archive/6.12/negroponte.html

"Being Digital also introduced the "Daily Me" concept of a virtual daily newspaper customized for an individual's tastes." –
http://en.wikipedia.org/wiki/Being_Digital

This concept is today called Flipboard an app that feeds your tablet all of your RSS Feeds to make a customized newspaper.

Paola Antonelli

Paola Antonelli is senior curator of architecture and design, and director of research and development, at the Museum of Modern Art (MoMA) in New York City. Her work investigates design's influence on everyday experience, often including overlooked objects and practices, and combining design, architecture, art, science, and technology. In addition to her role as senior curator of architecture and design at MoMA, Antonelli was appointed director of a new research and development initiative in 2012. She lectures frequently at high-level global conferences and coordinates cultural discussions at the World Economic Forum in Davos. A true interdisciplinary, energetic, and generous cultural thinker, Antonelli was recently rated as one of the top one hundred most powerful people in the world of art by Art Review.

- http://www.media.mit.edu/people/paolaa

First seeing Antonelli on The Colbert Report I instantly fell in love. Not physically, but mentally. Here was a person so respected in the art world whom also shared my belief. Probably saved years of therapy for me.

Below is part of an article by Antonelli from "The Economist" in 2010.

> *"There are still people who believe that design is just about making things, people and places pretty. In truth, design has spread like gas to almost all facets of human activity, from science and education to politics and policymaking. For a simple reason: one of design's most fundamental tasks is to help people deal with change.*
>
> *Designers stand between revolutions and everyday life. When the Internet happened, they created interfaces with buttons and hyperlinks that enabled us all to use it. Designers make disruptive innovations manageable and approachable, so that they can be embraced and assimilated into life. And they never forget functionality and elegance.*
>
> *In 25 years designers will be at the nexus of things. They will not be divvied up according to their reductive specialty (graphic, product, furniture, so 20th-century!). On the contrary, like physics, design will be loosely separated between theoretical and applied.*
>
> *Theoretical designers will be exquisite generalists—a bit like French philosophers, but ready to roll up their sleeves. Applied designers will visualise complex infrastructures and systems so that scientists, policymakers and the general public can manage and influence them; they will bring economy and common sense to the production of consumer goods.*
>
> *This grand new era has already begun. Design is moving centre-stage in the eternal human quest to make beauty out of necessity."*

> *http://www.economist.com/node/17509367*

After hearing her speak and reading these articles one can't help but think and hopefully realize how much design has come to the forefront of this century. The reason for that in Antonelli's opinion – *"one of design's most fundamental tasks is to help people deal with change."*

Can anyone think of a bigger time in history when so much change occurred in such little time, and the effect that change has had on society – at the basic core level of survival? Read some Robert Reich or Thomas Friedman to see how much these "changes" have affected the everyday lives of people.

The central point is - in my humble opinion – *"eternal human quest to make beauty out of necessity".* Now define beauty- because the question comes up - how do we define beauty? What does this have to do with the Digital Incunabula? Well, the goal of the five sectors discussed so far in this book is really connected to what we find beautiful, and is the core of beauty connected to necessity – to functionality.

So we go back to Hume versus Kant and at length Spinoza. No time for that now, but the basis of that argument is – is beauty found in objects innately or is it held to a standard of tastes? Tastes based on what? In my belief, it's based on whether or not the beauty adds to the human experience. And now to define the core of that experience, hopefully to function better within the society, in essence to survive better as a large community (Spinoza)... but that is another huge discussion.

To help understand that process I turn to John Maeda, Whitney Biennial artist, former President of RISD and currently Partner at Kleiner Perkins Caufield & Byers, and also Chair of the eBay Inc. Design Advisory Board.

John Maeda, Ph.D

John Maeda is Partner at Kleiner Perkins Caufield & Byers, and also Chair of the eBay Inc Design Advisory Board. He actively bridges technology, design, and leadership. His work *as an artist, graphic designer, computer scientist and educator earned him the distinction of being named one of the 75 most influential people of the 21st century by Esquire. As a professor at the MIT Media Lab starting in 1996, Maeda led research that brought together technologists, designers, and business leaders into a common space of possibility. Maeda's early work -- bridging advanced computation with traditional visual art -- is represented in the* permanent collection *of the Museum of Modern Art.* http://about.me/johnmaeda

In a recent NY Times article on the current disruptions Maeda states,

"We're on the tail end of technology being special," says John Maeda, *president of the Rhode Island School of Design. "The automobile was a weird alien technology when it first debuted, then, after a while, it evolved and designers stepped in to add value to it."*

Now, Mr. Maeda said, this shift has happened to technology, be it computers, smartphones or the iPad Mini.

"We have this exciting next step for design," he said. "Now that we have enough technology to do anything, design can now begin to be better than the technology itself."

http://bits.blogs.nytimes.com/2013/01/13/disruptions-design-to-propel-technology-forward/?_r=0

This to me is the crux f this new time to go from the "how" to the "why". Also in this next article Maeda describes his experience in the educational space, the future of digital integration into learning, and states some of the obstacles he has recently come across.

> "Maeda came to RISD from the MIT Media Lab with little administrative or fundraising experience in 2007. During his tenure, he has attempted to fold digital technology into the school's stubbornly analog approach to arts education, with mixed results. At one point, he earned a vote of no confidence from the faculty. At the same time, during the six years he's been at the head of the institution, the number of students applying to RISD has gone up, as have the number of financial aid packages offered, and tuition increases have been at their lowest in decades. In 2012, the school had a 97% job placement rate for graduates."

> http://www.fastcodesign.com/3023047/why-john-maeda-is-leaving-risd-for-a-venture-capital-firm

So here is one of the questions regarding the events surrounding Maeda's tenure at RISD, given his prior experience. Why would one of the oldest educational institutions - with literally the word "Design" in its name - not heed the advice of someone like Maeda? Obviously we are in a time of extreme shifts and changes. So why not listen to someone who has in all probability seen these changes up close and personal and bridged the obstacles beforehand? And if individuals let that confusion guide their principals then how many others are being affected by this avoidance? How many others are having their future decided by the same individuals that families have entrusted their life savings and their children's future?

There have been record drops in enrollments at private universities in the past five years. The traditional state university systems have seen huge surges in enrollment, due primarily to price difference. So it would seem that in order to maintain their position in the marketplace these private schools would need to answer the $100,000.00 difference question. Many do, but it seems in the case of RISD and other privates that question still looms.

So with the apparent disruptions and the possibility of such potential innovation, why not adopt a different perspective? It seems some schools have invested in the difference, this opinion is coming from Dr. Maeda, whose perspective is based on industry as well as academia.

David Kelley

> In 1978, David co-founded the design firm that ultimately became IDEO. Today, he serves as chair of IDEO and is the Donald W. Whittier Professor at Stanford, where he has taught for more than 25 years. Preparing the design thinkers of tomorrow earned David the Sir Misha Black Medal for his "distinguished contribution to design education."

"I was sitting at a big dinner in Pacific Heights recently, and I told my hostess I was a designer.

'Oh,' she said. 'So what do you think of my curtains?" That, Kelley says, is not where we're going.

And a quote from Kelley from the same article:

*"We moved from thinking of ourselves as designers to thinking of our-selves as **design thinkers**. We have a methodology that enables us to come up with a **solution** that nobody has before." — David Kelley - http://www.fastcompany.com/1139331/ideos-david-kelley-design-thinking*

d.school at Stanford is built similar to IDEO's structure. Here is a description of the structure from their website.

Students come to the d.school with an intense curiosity, a deep affinity for other people, and the desire to gain an understanding beyond their own experience. They come from every school on campus, and beyond. Instead of working on different pieces of the same project, they navigate each step in the innovation process together, leveraging their differences as a kind of creative engine. The design thinking process becomes a glue that holds teams together, allowing students to unleash intuitive leaps, lateral think-ing, and new ways of looking at old problems.

- http://dschool.stanford.edu/our-point-of-view/#design-thinking

To me this combination of diverse users and designers, and developers is the perfect blend in academia towards the profession Kelley and IDEO's influence on the world cannot be overstated. As one of the original designers hired by Steve Jobs and many others, Kelley evokes the process of change with every assignment he and his company IDEO undertakes. This new concept of "design thinkers" is to me the basis for the next century of design and innovation. Gathering a group together in order to make the design process Kelley and Maeda evoke, creates a new structure and a new order for a new century. A new structure that in my opinion is well placed to deal with the opportunities and crisis that will surely come as part of the Digital Incunabula.

As stated before this new approach to design study and the subsequent pro-cesses that have evolved are in some schools with that focus being entitled "Interaction Design".

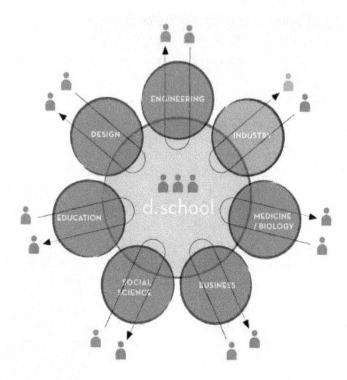

The figure above is also from the dschool site.

Interaction Design

Interaction Design is now becoming not just a "buzzword" or "industry jargon" as some design academics likes to call it but obviously a real driving force behind changes in that discipline.

Here is a description from some schools as to the focus of their curriculum.

> *The MFA in Interaction Design program trains students to research, analyze, prototype, and design concepts in their business, social, and cultural contexts.*
>
> *The two-year graduate program explores the strategic role of interaction design in shaping everyday life, and intends to increase the relevancy of design to business and society so designers can make a difference. It seeks to cultivate interaction design as a discipline and further its visibility as a community of practice.*
>
> *Where we stand in the history of the future is a tremendous opportunity for the design of interactions. We invite all to participate as students, as teachers, as collaborators, and as citizens." -*
> *http://interactiondesign.sva.edu/*

These sorts of changes in academia in my opinion do not reflect a short arc or transition but a major re-focusing. Here is a short excerpt and a short list of other institutions focusing on "Interaction Design" as both an undergraduate and graduate major.

Many academic institutions with new or established interaction design and HCI programs are beginning to develop an understanding of interaction design and the qualities and skills required of interaction designers. Some of the most forward-thinking of these institutions include:

- *Carnegie Mellon University*

- *Institute of Design, Illinois Institute of Technology*

- *North Carolina State University*

- *University of Art and Design Helsinki*

- *Virginia Commonwealth University*

- http://www.cooper.com/journal/2008/05/so_you_want_to_be_an_interacti

Is all education feeling the effect of these disruptions and the need for a re-design? Is it the schools concern only? Well not according to Sir Ken Robinson.

Sir Ken Robinson

Professor Emeritus of Education Warwick University

Senior advisor J. Paul Getty Trust Los Angeles

Author, speaker and workshop leader

"Sir Ken Robinson, PhD is an internationally recognized leader in the development of creativity, innovation and human resources in education and in business. He is also one of the world's leading speakers on these topics, with a profound impact on audiences everywhere. The videos of his famous 2006 and 2010 talks to the prestigious TED Conference have been viewed more than 25 million times and seen by an estimated 250 million people in over 150 countries. His 2006 talk is the most viewed in TED's history. In 2011 he was listed as "one of the world's elite thinkers on creativity and innovation" by Fast Company magazine, and was ranked among the Thinkers50 list of the world's top business thought leaders." - http://sirkenrobinson.com/about-2/

Next are just some of his views on the future of education and the world. In my opinion he is truly one of the best minds in modern day education and the use of technology to improve that experience.

Economically and culturally, the future of America and of the rest of world lies now in a different direction. It will depend on the vitality, diversity and creativity of all its people. The good news is that there are many strong, practical and highly effective new forms of education that point the way. In future blogs, I'll say what some of the best of these are and the basic principles on which they're based.

... The wholesale transformation of education is at the heart of the changes that are needed. It's not something that Congress, or the state governments, can get round to later on. If they put this off for too long, they may find that that they and the whole country are left behind. - http://www.huffingtonpost.com/sir-ken-robinson/transform-education-yes-w_b_157014.html

A lot of Robinson's points are what I try to reflect in class discussions. But here are more of his viewpoints in simplified form since what he has to say needs well, an entire book.

> *"The fact is that given the challenges we face, education doesn't need to be reformed -- it needs to be transformed. The key to this transformation is not to standardize education, but to personalize it, to build achievement on discovering the individual talents of each child, to put students in an environment where they want to learn and where they can naturally discover their true passions."*
> *— Ken Robinson, The Element: How Finding Your Passion Changes Everything*

A very poignant and funny viewpoint I share on this new generation, the one I refer to as Gen-I (Generation Interactive – my next book BTW).

> *"When my son, James, was doing homework for school, he would have five or six windows open on his computer, Instant Messenger was flashing continuously, his cell phone was constantly ringing, and he was downloading music and watching the TV over his shoulder. I don't know if he was doing any homework, but he was running an empire as far as I could see, so I didn't really care." — Ken Robinson, The Element: How Finding Your Passion Changes Everything*

What is the current state of education and where should it be reformed or simply evolved into current needs? Robinson always reflects back on the early days of industrialization lifestyle that created our modern day educational system and how that needs to change. This quote from Robinson seems to share the belief of Brynjolfsson.

"Public schools were not only created in the interests of industrialism—they were created in the image of industrialism. In many ways, they reflect the factory culture they were designed to support."
— *Ken Robinson, The Element: How Finding Your Passion Changes Everything*

And what is the future of education and where should it be going in this new age of digital reformation and delivery of content?

"One of the essential problems for education is that most countries subject their schools to the fast-food model of quality assurance when they should be adopting the Michelin model instead. The future for education is not in standardizing but in customizing; not in promoting groupthink and "deindividuation" but in cultivating the real depth and dynamism of human abilities of every sort."
— *Ken Robinson, The Element: How Finding Your Passion Changes Everything*

Summary

As a summary to this chapter I thought it necessary to tie this a bit together. Why try to relate all of these diverse areas of influences and priorities?

As Antonelli says, *"In truth, design has spread like gas to almost all facets of human activity, from science and education to politics and policymaking. For a simple reason: one of design's most fundamental tasks is to help people deal with change."*

This is why I instantly fell in love. For someone as respected, intelligent, and successful as Antonelli to be saying that all of these areas of society are tied together through the practice and concept of design truly helped validate my beliefs as well. Everything needs to be designed in order to function properly for the human. Some may think innate design, as by a supernatural being (or just Steve Jobs - close enough I guess) – but a purpose or plan is usually in place. And please remember, when the word design is used we are not talking about curtains or khaki or beige... we are simply talking about – from Problem to Solution.

Chapter 6 - The ripple reformation

When ripples are strong enough they can push objects into small groupings. Undersea life, and anything else in the path of these ripples, sort of gather together. These gatherings can be forced or formed due to where the items start or where their weight has re-positioned them. Nevertheless, they are there and seem now to go together. Maybe it's more ideal to see how they can work together, instead of trying to reposition them as they were. Maybe the next ripple will simply send them back to those points again.

As jobs fall from the bottom and the top, the middle level jobs become basically the arena for the "Hunger Games". Think about it, the person who used to do printing is now pushed out and looking for a similar salary level. And they just keep pushing down and around. Further and further down.

Specifically in the print/publishing industry, individuals in all of these positions had to push towards other industries:

- Editorial Designer
- Editor/Assistant editor
- Typesetter
- Proofreader
- Photographer
- Camera lab technician
- Camera operator
- Film stripper
- Plate maker

- Press operator

- Printer/Printer's Devil – assistant

- Edition Collator

- Forklift operator

- Delivery truck driver – mechanic

- Jumper – delivery assistant

- Warehouse manager and workers

- Paper companies – entire staff and facility

- Ink manufacturers – entire staff and facility

- Lumber industry – dramatic drop in need for paper and products

- And on and on...

Now apply that metric to industries that produce traditional analog products in information, entertainment, promotion, education, and the arts. The drop-off of jobs from this Digital Incunabula is astounding.

For years I was asked at speaking engagements, "Who can make this transition?" and I had to provide an indirect answer. I would say if you worked hard and studied you could apply your skills and knowledge to this new era. The fact was – and is – not many will make the transition. Why? Because they simply weren't trained to think this new way and im my opinion this goes right along with what Brynjolfsson argues.

> *"We have an educational system designed for a 20th century economy,"* *says Brynjolfsson, "with students trained to memorize and follow instructions and rules, an approach initially designed to prepare them for factory work that today is largely mechanized."*

We are still teaching the how-to world. And in the case of design – my discipline – we are still doing demos on how to use software. The problem is that the students have accelerated way beyond that level – especially with services like YouTube and Lynda.com (recently purchased by LinkedIn for $1.9 billion dollars.)They have these skills coming out of High School. I'm not saying to give up the how-to's... just moderate them down to a quicker, smaller part of the semester. My belief is the same as Brynjolfsson.

> *Instead, Brynjolfsson argues for an emphasis on creative thinking and problem-solving skills that will enable students to go on to the sorts of jobs that can only be done by humans – and tend to offer higher financial and emotional rewards as well.*

Again with moderation, not complete theory but how that theory is applied, based on determining the needs of the problem – essentially true design.

Well what are examples of these attempts at re-design? In the next section we will be discussing the attempts at reformation and re-design in each of the six sectors.

Information reforms

The information sector in order to survive, whether it is industry journals or newspapers to basic information like dictionaries, encyclopedias, product reviews, cooking recipes, television listings, car manuals and even maps. Many, if not all of these entities, have made the move to a digital platform. In making this transition many have found the virtue of a paperless structure. Why bother to discuss this? Well, before anyone takes a step in a college direction or new career path, you should know whether that limb is stable and safe.

In this section I will provide samples of some popular forms of transformation like switching to online, app development, and a new term - content "curation".

Switch to web-based

How many typical information sources have now stopping printing and switched to online distribution? Magazines and newspapers alone have seen plummeting readership, but also has traditional platforms like dictionaries and encyclopedias. What happened to the business of news and information? Here is a snippet of an amazing report from Pew Research.

State of the News Media 2014

By Amy Mitchell

> ***Overview***
>
> *In many ways, 2013 and early 2014 brought a level of energy to the news industry not seen for a long time. Even as challenges of the past several years continue and new ones emerge, the activities this year have created a new sense of optimism – or perhaps hope – for the future of American journalism.*
>
> -   *http://www.journalism.org/2014/03/26/state-of-the-news-media-2014-overview/*

App and smartphone adaptations

Apps are obviously one of the fastest growing areas for all information retrieval, but this is not to say that's where it stops. They are basically replacing the delivery of content that was previously produced through traditional formats and expanding those capabilities. How many news and information sources now have apps for your mobile devices? How many apps are there for just simple everyday life needs?

In a recent article on Techhive.com you can find the top 10 apps that replace typical products to create and store your information, from digital "paper pads" to the "Yellow Pages" to the "Oxford Dictionary". I have selected just a few examples.

Think for just a moment how much of a disruptive effect using a "digital pad" is to the paper industry. How many notebooks and legal pads have you purchased, touched, or used in your lifetime? How many people are employed in the paper manufacturing industry, not to mention the office supply business?

Moleskine

If you keep a paper notepad in your bag, replace it with the Moleskine app for your iPad and iPhone. You can choose plain, ruled, or squared paper style.

The app has a sketching tool, and you can geotag and share your notes via email or over social networks. Available for iPad, iPhone, and iPod Touch.

Very short and abridged list below:

Yellow Pages

Oxford Dictionary

Papers

http://www.techhive.com/article/241198/top_10_ipad_and_iphone_paper_re placement_apps.html

With 100,000s of apps available I guess the current mantra is true – "there's an app for that!" is soon going to apply for everything we need.

Maps and Manuals

To understand the impact of switching to online for companies that produce maps or manuals, just do a simple Google search for "owners manual" and see how many sites come up. Everything you could think of is listed from home appliances to luxury yachts. Every item has a website and a manual associated with it – and many have how-to videos as well.

When was the last time you asked a person for directions to anything, anywhere? When was the last time you actually bought tickets in paper form to a game or event? When was the last time you read the newspaper for a restaurant review? When was the last time you *needed* to?

How has this changed the landscape? In some ways it has stayed the same – writers still have to write the words, pictures are still needed, but now video production teams need to be involved. The "how-to" marketplace is exploding on YouTube and other video content delivery platforms. A great example of a quick, simple way to organize your needs has been through the evolution and explosion of the use of the Internet as a base for content-curation.

Pinterest is a great example. You laugh? Well, so did many people at first. Here is an excerpt from a New York magazine article based on how many felt that way at first.

"It's Time to Start Taking Pinterest Seriously

> *Three years after its founding, Pinterest is not only thriving, but beating lots of other popular Internet companies where it counts. The site just raised $225 million at a valuation of $3.8 billion — making it worth fifteen times as much as the Washington Post, twice as much as the New York Times, and more than Spotify, as of its last closed funding round. So why was I until recently — and why do others still seem to be — unwilling to take Pinterest as seriously as those businesses?- http://nymag.com/daily/intelligencer/2013/10/time-to-start-taking-pinterest-seriously.html*

Other forms of quick content-curation are being developed and assimilated into everyday use with sites like Curata.

4 Reasons Why Content Curation Has Gone Mainstream

Guest post written by Pawan Deshpande

Pawan Deshpande is CEO of Curata.

> *With the help of Pinterest and other consumer-oriented companies, content curation – the process of finding, organizing and sharing online content – has gone mainstream. More and more people are looking to content curation to help them navigate today's chaotic online world. But it's not only consumers that are benefitting.*

> *http://www.forbes.com/sites/ciocentral/2012/06/04/4-reasons-why-content-curation-has-gone-mainstream/*

So why is this so important in the area of information reformation? Because as the ripples affect the playing field those little boats – viewers and users – drift and move with the ripples.

Remember what the late Yogi Berra said, "That place is too busy. Nobody goes there anymore."

Publishing reforms

In the publishing sector, a move towards the distributing of content through digital platforms has been at best slow and at worst tricky. Legal issues surrounding intellectual property rights have popped up in court like Meer Kats smelling a predator. Not to mention the never-ending question – "how do you make money on the web?"

Many traditional publications have decided to try numerous avenues to profitability. Some of them are:

- Paywalls
- Dual membership – print and digital
- Advertiser sponsorship
- Digital editions

How have these reformations fared?

<u>Online Magazines and Digital Editions</u>

The fall and rise of magazines from print to digital

Declining sales do not mean the end for glossies. More platforms mean better ways of connecting people with their passions

Challenging times lie ahead for magazines. The Audit Bureau of Circulations figures published last month made grim reading. Sales of celebrity titles, such as Heat, Hello! and Closer have plummeted, squeezed out by celebrity websites and the Daily Mail's sidebar of shame. Weekly women's consumer titles and Nuts's miserable year-on-year sales figures (-29.7%) merely confirmed the downward spiral. Even NME stalwarts seem to be abandoning their weekly fix (down 16.6%).

http://www.theguardian.com/media-network/media-network-blog/2013/mar/07/fall-rise-magazines-print-digital

This area of discussion could produce about a million research links, but we all know the answer. Just ask yourself these questions.

When was the last time you opened your mailbox and found a magazine?

When was the last time you ran out to "get the papers, get the papers?"

When was the last time your child sold magazine subscriptions for school?

You get the picture, now here are some that kind of say it all.

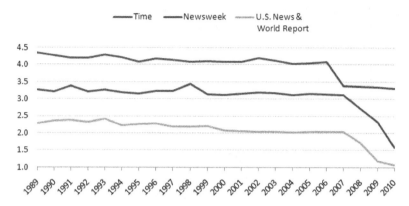

Time Circulation Holds Steady in 2010

In Millions

Source: Audit Bureau of Circulations, FAS-FAX report for consumer magazines
PEW RESEARCH CENTER'S PROJECT FOR EXCELLENCE IN JOURNALISM
2011 STATE OF THE NEWS MEDIA

<u>Paywalls and Dual Subscriptions for Specific Devices</u>

Paywalls Versus Advertising? Why Not Both?

Publishers debate the viability of paywalls at DPAC.

Advertising and paywalls are typically viewed as a mutually exclusive proposition but they can successfully co-exist, according to participants at a roundtable at <u>DPAC</u> *(Digital Publishing and Advertising Conference) this week.*

"Why not dual models?" said Andrew Rutledge, vice president and general manager of publisher development at<u>PubMatic</u>. "Who's paying for digital content from more than two providers? The market can only support two or three players with a paywall. I don't think the paywall is THE solution, it's one of many."

Paying for Content or for Access on a Select Device?

The panelists cited News Corp.'s The Daily and The New York Times as two publishers taking different approaches to paid content-with The Daily only available on select devices, while The New York Times is charging for content across a <u>variety of platforms</u>. "Is the value simply that you can access it on the iPad?" said Hecht. "Or is there some functionality that makes it different? How do you keep The Daily from being just a novelty item?

- <u>http://www.foliomag.com/2011/paywalls-versus-advertising-why-not-both/</u>

Turnabout is Fare Play

Some magazines that boasted of not having paid advertisers quickly changed their tune once they headed for the Web. One typical example is that when PC Mag was in print, it didn't have ads, but once they were sold from Ziff Davis the website is now full of software and hardware ads.

I witnessed this first hand with regional papers like Newsday's transformation to newsday.com. As part of the consulting group brought in to start the re-design it was always evident how different and difficult this new payment model was going to be in this new space.

Below is a screenshot of the pcmag.com homepage on Jan. 21, 2015, ironically showing an article about how worthless Google ads are for publishers. And below that a chart on what may have caused such a demise.

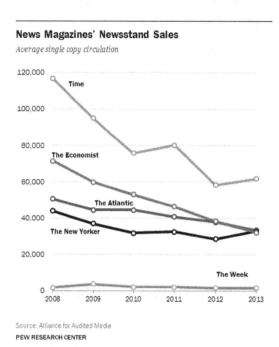

News Magazines' Newsstand Sales

Average single copy circulation

Source: Alliance for Audited Media

PEW RESEARCH CENTER

Google Books

Google Books originated as a project in Google Labs, which has since tran-spired into an arm of Google that makes millions of books available for viewing on the web for free. Now information can be accessed for free from anywhere - without leaving your home - and can also be searchable. No more Dewey Deci-mal system, no more wooden drawers to fumble with, no more searching and searching only to find the book has been checked out and never returned.

This move was huge for publishing and information reformation. And one that opened up some huge litigation. Here is an excerpt from an article on Reu-ters.com about the recent lawsuit won by Google.

"Google defeats authors in U.S. book-scanning lawsuit

By Jonathan Stempel

> *(Reuters) - Google Inc on Thursday won dismissal of a long-running law-suit by authors who accused the Internet search company of digitally copy-ing millions of books for an online library without permission.*
>
> *U.S. Circuit Judge Denny Chin in Manhattan accepted Google's argument that its scanning of more than 20 million books, and making "snippets" of text available online, constituted "fair use" under U.S. copyright law.*
>
> *The decision, if it survives an expected appeal, would let Google continue expanding the library, which it said helps readers find books they might not otherwise locate.*

It is also turning point for litigation that began in 2005, when authors and publishers sued. Google has estimated it could owe more than $3 billion if the Authors Guild, an advocacy group that demanded $750 for each scanned book, prevailed. -http://www.reuters.com/article/2013/11/14/us-google-books-idUSBRE9AD0TT20131114

Now, how to make this information easily accessible without dragging around a laptop or being tethered to a desktop station?

Books versus Nooks, iPads and Kindles

There is so much debate on this topic it could fill a book. Bad joke, but had to use it. I personally can't believe the discussion about this topic. Here is my two-cents worth, like anything, the question is what are you using the information for? If I wanted to sit down and have an alcoholic drink it would matter what it was for. If it's during a meal I'd probably choose wine, if it was out on the town I'd likely ask for a scotch. And if I wanted to get seriously drunk probably tequila.

Kind of similar to reading (that was a stretch but I do find knowledge intoxicating) - if I want to find information fast – digital. If I wanted to lounge around and just browse, or have coffee and relax I'd probably choose a traditional paper book. But if I was in school and had to carry five books to and from class – a digital solution makes sense. Like all good design, the first question is "what is the problem?" and then find the solution.

Here's an article from of all places the Financial Times on eBooks versus Print books.

"On the other side of the two cultures divide, the novelist and critic Will Self recently argued that the connectivity of the digital world was fatal for the serious novel, which requires all the reader's attention. Looking ahead 20 years, he posed a question: "If you accept that by then the vast majority of text will be read in digital form on devices linked to the web, do you also believe that those readers will voluntarily choose to disable that connectivity? If your answer to this is no, then the death of the novel is sealed out of your own mouth."

E-reading is certainly on the rise. The Pew Research Center reports that, as recently as 2010, hardly anyone in the US had an e-reader or tablet. Now half do. The proportion of the population who have read an ebook in the past year rose from 17 per cent in 2011 to 28 per cent just three years later. In the UK, figures from Nielsen, which monitors book sales, showed that one in four consumer titles bought in 2013 was an ebook, up from one in five a year earlier."

http://www.ft.com/cms/s/2/53d3096a-f792-11e3-90fa-00144feabdc0.html

There is so much discussion in this area still. Digital Editions of magazines, a plethora of Frankenstein-like reanimated malformed objects and incarnations.

It reminds me of when we used to try to put our kids down for bedtime. The fights, the struggles, the "just one more glass of water" delays... We all knew it was bedtime, but being children they just kept trying to put off the inevitable. The same is true now for the days of paper publishing and distribution.

Promotion reforms

In the promotion and advertising sector the world has turned upside down and back again. Don Draper would just be sitting at the conference table doing shots of scotch until he passed out. Everything from the creative process, to the strategy session, to the client meeting is just completely different - and most of the strategy seems radically absurd in comparison. Not to mention the effects of social media marketing.

The gut instinct of the 1950-80's is gone. No company or agency can afford today to be wrong. Everything is about efficiency of operations.

Here is an excerpt of the creative process from an article in Adweek.

"Gary Koepke, chief creative officer for North America at SapientNitro, said he values the notion of "connected thinking," and invites all sorts of people from across the agency to come to brainstorming meetings—even people not with the agency.

"Ultimately what I like is the random molecule idea," he said. "Invite someone who maybe has nothing to do with anything. Maybe it's an artist or a musician. Maybe it's my mom. Anybody to say, 'Why are you doing that?' or 'What's this?' or 'You guys always do the same thing.' I believe everybody is creative, so it doesn't matter who's in the room, as long as they've been briefed properly and somebody is managing that process."

You also have to listen—really listen—Koepke added. "Ideas hide within a sentence somebody says, or a phrase, or a combination of words they write down that you might not be paying attention to," he said. "These ideas are very fleeting as well. Always write these things down so they don't get away from you. Keep them close to you." Finally, Koepke added, give your ideas room to breathe.

... Reid Miller, ecd at Taxi in New York, the final panelist, spoke about his agency's move from a linear process of ideation (client -> account -> strategy -> creative -> idea) to a more circular one, where staffers from all disciplines surround the idea and add to it. This helps make the idea bigger across the different media (TV, print, digital, out of home, etc.) rather than having small cookie-cutter iterations of the same idea mindless tailored to each one.

At the core of idea generation, he added, is curiosity.

"Everybody in this circle has to be curious," he said. "And what curious means is three things: You have to be curious and doubt what you know. You want to learn and take in new information constantly. Curiosity also means collaboration—a desire to work with all these different people who

have a completely different point of view on the problem than you do. And last, curiosity also means being able to change—change what you thought you knew, change what you thought worked, and add to that. Take what you've done in the past, and put all the little pieces together and build a bigger idea."

"We used to talk about peeling the onion," Miller concluded. "Today it's about building—layer upon layer upon layer upon layer, until suddenly you see you have a big idea."

- http://www.adweek.com/news/advertising-branding/genius-or-process-how-top-creative-directors-come-great-ideas-152697

Still the same in effect but now let's move that to the strategy. How do the available vehicles change the creative? Here from Forbes:

4 Principles of Marketing Strategy In The Digital Age

Life for marketers used to be simpler. We had just a few TV channels, some radio stations, a handful of top magazines and a newspaper or two in each market. Reaching consumers was easy, if you were able craft a compelling message, you could move product.

Ugh! Now we've got a whole slew of TV channels, millions of web sites and hundreds of thousands of "Apps" along with an alphabet soup of DMP's, API's and SDK's. Marketing was never easy, but technology has made it a whole lot tougher.

What used to be a matter of identifying needs and communicating benefits now requires us to build immersive experiences that engage consumers. That means we have to seamlessly integrate a whole new range of skills and capabilities. It's easy to get lost among a sea of buzzwords and _false gurus_ selling snake oil. Here are 4 principles to guide you:

- **Clarify Business Objectives**

- **Use Innovation Teams to Identify, Evaluate and Activate Emerging Opportunities**

- **Decouple Strategy and Innovation**

- **Build Open Assets in the Marketplace**
  - http://www.forbes.com/sites/gregsatell/2013/04/16/4-principles-of-marketing-strategy-in-the-digital-age/

Analytics versus gut instinct

"Should Tech Designers Go With Their Guts — Or the Data?

When it comes to the future of design and technology, the uncomfortable question we bump into is: do human design instincts even matter anymore?

In the design world, there's always been a dichotomy between data and instinct. Design departments — think Mad Men — were once driven by the belief that some people are gifted with an innate design sense. They glorified gut "instinct" because it was extremely difficult to measure the effectiveness of designs in progress; designers had to wait until a product shipped to learn if their ideas were any good. But today's digital products — think Facebook and Google — glorify "data" instead; it's now possible to measure each design element among hundreds of variations until the perfect outcome is selected.

For designers, this influx of data can be frustrating.

Designers who thought they were hired for their good taste will quickly get discouraged in a culture where tech companies meticulously test 41 shades of blue. Imagine convincing a team to trust your gut instincts when cold hard data says you're wrong. How do you simplify a crowded homepage when the data scientists agree it's ugly, but tell you it signs up customers faster?" - http://www.wired.com/2013/11/design-world-stop-fighting-over-data-vs-instinct/

And here is my point about design, if its main purpose is to sell the product why would a true "designer" suggest a different solution? After all of this pondering and strategy choices it has seemed to come down to the basics – how to get attention amidst the clutter. View-ability = Measuring (the right) eyeballs!

The Trouble With 'Viewability' as a Metric for Digital Ads

It's a Step in the Right Direction, but Imprecise and Potentially Costly

One of the great challenges of digital advertising is getting assurance that users actually see the ads for which the advertisers are paying. Traditional print media has its problems, but buying page 6 of the September issue of Vogue pretty much guarantees eyeballs. It's not the same in digital.

New metrics and standards have cropped up trying to solve this problem. In some circles the idea of the viewable impression has gained steam: measuring an ad's length of viewability as a proxy for determining the likelihood that it has been seen. Yet the metric of viewability brings troubles of its own.

Joshua Koran, formerly with AT&T AdWorks, wrote recently that the metric will not help, in part because sellers will increase prices to make up for the money lost on unviewable and thus unpaid-for impressions. Such padding would drive up costs across the board." - http://adage.com/article/digitalnext/trouble-viewability-a-metric-digital-ads/237815/

Social Media Marketing Effect

The effect of social media platforms on promotion and marketing cannot and should not be understated. Since 2004 when Facebook debuted the effect of community on products and brands has been felt. In the early days friends would ask me "what is Twitter?" and "why should I care?" My response on platforms like Twitter, Instagram, Tumblr, and Pinterest has been this – no one will care what you are eating or where you ate it. But YOU will care if your favorite restaurant, car dealership, clothing store has a preferred customer sale. I tell them - corporations believe the line - it's not YOU it's ME.

Again Nielsen comes into the discussion. See below for an excerpt on the subject.

"Research shows that social media is increasingly a platform consumers use to express their loyalty to their favorite brands and products, and many seek to reap benefits from brands for helping promote their products. Among those who share their brand experiences through social media, at least 41 percent say they do so to receive discounts. When researching products, social media users are likely to trust the recommendations of their friends and family most, and results from Nielsen's Global Online Survey indicate that 2 out of 3 respondents said they were either highly or somewhat influenced by advertising with a social context.

Social Media also plays a key role in protecting brands: 58 percent of social media users say they write product reviews to protect others from bad experiences, and nearly 1 in 4 say they share their negative experiences to "punish companies". Many customers also use social media to engage with brands on a customer service level, with 42 percent of 18- to 34-year-olds acknowledging that they expect customer support within 12 hours of a complaint." - http://www.nielsen.com/us/en/insights/news/2011/how-social-media-impacts-brand-marketing.html*

Measuring the performance

Now that it's all done, you simply have to sit back and wait for the results. In many of these cases it's like a tough series of blood tests, with possibly the same results. And the same name you have known for years is still doing the job.

"Nielsen Online Campaign Ratings provides a comprehensive, next-day view of your ad's online and mobile audience in a way comparable to the Nielsen TV ratings. Powered by the largest user databases and the highest quality panel in the world, Nielsen Online Campaign Ratings set a new industry standard for digital audience measurement." - http://www.nielsen.com/campaignratings.html*

Now with all of this going on - and considering this applies to the world of print, television, radio and online - hopefully the depth of the effect of this new Digital Incunabula is apparent.

Teaching design and especially advertising takes on a whole new idiom and scope. Gone are the days when just "sex sells" and "free this or that" will get the job done. This new structure has changed the game for good. And in my opinion it is our job as teachers of design to properly prepare students for that change – everyday.

Entertainment reforms

As stated before, the Digital Incunabula hit the entertainment sector the hardest. The music segment specifically was completely turned upside down by the change in the economic model of delivery and selection. Attempts at reforming the model did involve some very drastic changes and solutions. In this section I will attempt to briefly list some of the solutions.

Licensing content

In an attempt to forge a partnership with these new platforms the music, television and movie industries have been forging partnerships and in some cases developing their own platforms for downloading and streaming content. Some of the biggest players in this space are:

- Amazon Prime
- Hulu
- iTunes
- Netflix
- Pandora
- Spotify

Second and third screen

Even the networks have started to embrace the world of online distribution with their own websites by allowing free play. They realize that they are losing viewership to a second screen - and a third - and who knows what else is coming up. Each platform has its own peccadillos and a big fear of cannibalizing existing profits from traditional venues and viewership has most traditional distribution schemes sometimes in a state of analysis paralysis.

Some of the discussion concerning these new aberrations is spoken about daily in the trade publications and even your typical news sources.

"Fewer People Than Ever Are Watching TV

People are watching more online video on their computers, smart TVs and multimedia devices

The long-prognosticated death of TV may be happening before our eyes— but at a glacial pace. A new in-depth report from tracking firm Nielsen shows that TV is still by far America's favorite entertainment past-time, but individuals are spending more hours surfing web and viewing streaming services. A growing number of households are choosing to dump TV altogether." - *http://time.com/3615387/tv-viewership-declining-nielsen/*

US TV-advert buyers hold back as viewers move online

The US television industry has just suffered the first decline in early advertising-buying since the recession. At this year's upfront market – the summer sales process in which networks typically sell about two-thirds of their commercial inventory to big brands for the coming TV season – spending fell 6 per cent to $18.1bn, according to Media Dynamics estimates. This is the first annual drop in upfront ad sales across broadcast and cable networks since 2009." - *http://www.ft.com/cms/s/0/edf1df26-2a32-11e4-8139-00144feabdc0.html#ixzz3Op2GohNX*

NBC Surprised as HBO, CBS Make Move to Online-Only Television

By Doni Bloomfield Oct 23, 2014 11:33 AM ET

Online-only TV came on faster than NBCUniversal was expecting.

Steve Burke, chief executive officer of the broadcaster owned by Comcast Corp. (CMCSA), was taken aback by the announcements last week that HBO and CBS are offering online-only services that don't require a cable subscription, he said in an investor call this morning.

"I was surprised," Burke said. "CBS I was surprised because they've been such a defender of retransmission consent and the traditional ecosystem and been so successful in the broadcast business. And HBO, because I think it's going to be such a challenge for them to not cannibalize what is already a really, really good business." - *http://www.bloomberg.com/news/2014-10-23/nbc-surprised-as-hbo-cbs-make-move-to-online-only-television.html*

ESPN will be available through a streaming service, no cable required

"For many TV viewers, the only reason to keep paying for expensive cable subscriptions is to watch sports. And for that, they invariably need ESPN, the powerful network that has exclusive rights to many of the country's most popular football and basketball games.

Now, that linchpin is being removed. For the first time ever, sports fans will be able to watch ESPN's programming streamed online to their tablets, laptops, smartphones and TVs—all without paying a cable or satellite bill." - *http://www.washingtonpost.com/news/business/wp/2015/01/05/espn-goes-streaming-through-dishs-sling-tv-no-cable-required/*

As was stated before movie industry is seeing its worst summer season in forever, music has been decimated sine the iPod launched, and radio had to reinvent itself like the wristwatch industry – Apple Watch2 coming out soon!

With this entire shift happening in music, radio, movies, and television how could educators not see the need for such a strong inclusion of digital assets and effects in curriculum? Why would anyone choose to walk away from such irrefutable evidence? I have always believed in the Vidal Sasson credo, *"if you don't look good, we don't look good"*. In other words if our students don't have the necessary skills both theoretical and applicable then how does that reflect back on the value proposition of education?

<u>Hipsters and hiccups – a return to vinyl</u>

But the hipsters are trying to keep the faith alive! Some entertainers are trying to return to vinyl and capture a new audience. Performers like Jack White and Neil Young are cutting live albums on the stage of the *Tonight Show starring Jimmy Fallon.*

> *"After the interview, Young hopped inside the box to perform "Crazy," a cover of Willie Nelson's 1961 hit popularized by Patsy Cline. Young, White, Fallon and guest Louis C.K. listened to the vinyl later in the show. Young also performed "Since I Met You Baby," a cover of R&B singer Ivory Joe Hunter's 1956 song, on piano while sitting inside the booth. That performance didn't make it to air, but was posted online by The Tonight Show."* - http://www.rollingstone.com/music/videos/neil-young-jack-white-cut-vinyl-record-live-on-tonight-show-20140513#ixzz3Op8rHqvI

Such stunts are a new way of using these shifts to get public relations moving. Whether you actually believe in what they are doing or not, in all good advertising you try to find a hook or event. Hucksters are hucksters are hucksters, even if they are using their superpowers for good instead of evil.

This reminds me of a great bit of dialogue from *Moonrise Kingdom* where an errant arrow kills a pet Scottish terrier, and the boy and girl find him.

Girl: "Was he a good dog?"

Boy: "Who's to say?"

Education reforms

In the education sector reform has been slow, then dramatic and with solutions that shake the pillars. These solutions have been structured via curriculum, methodology and have been implemented through both hardware and software.

As discussed before the areas of reformation have been:

- Common Core
- Tablets in the classroom
- Use of the Internet as a learning tool
- eTextbooks
- Gen-I
- STEM & STEAM
- MOOCs

One area of dramatic change and tremendous scrutiny is the Common Core. This is not being met with the acceptance and rational discussion that was hoped for when started. The reason I bring up Common Core is to show how almost any initiative gets twisted and turned until it slowly dies. To me these changes can be more easily integrated with the use of technology to display and to allow for further review and discussion This way all stakeholders can witness the progress. Again, this is a way for the Digital Incunabula to aid in transformation on a national scale easily and affordably.

Common Core

According to the Common Core Standards website this definition is given regarding the initiative.

> *The Common Core is a set of high-quality academic standards in mathematics and English language arts/literacy (ELA). These learning goals outline what a student should know and be able to do at the end of each grade. The standards were created to ensure that all students graduate from high school with the skills and knowledge necessary to succeed in college, career, and life, regardless of where they live. Forty-three states, the District of Columbia, four territories, and the Department of Defense Education Activity (DoDEA) have voluntarily adopted and are moving forward with the Common Core. –*

http://www.corestandards.org/about-the-standards/

*The Common Core, the <u>most significant change</u> to American public edu-
cation in a generation, was hailed by the Obama administration as a way
of lifting achievement at low-performing schools. After decades of rote
learning, children would become nimble thinkers equipped for the modern age, capable of unraveling improper fractions and drawing connec-
tions between Lincoln and Pericles.*

<u>http://www.nytimes.com/2014/06/15/education/common-core-in-9-
year-old-eyes.html?_r=0</u>

And whether or not Common Core support and opposition is merely a
political battle?

*"People who study these issues have wrestled for decades or even centu-
ries with the question of when public views change or when politics change,
is that because it's bubbling up from the bottom or because leaders are acting and that's trickling down?" Hess, director of education policy studies at
AEI, says. "I think the answer is usually some of each."*

<u>http://www.usnews.com/news/articles/2014/09/26/common-core-
controversy-is-it-all-politics</u>

<u>Just a new revenue stream?</u>

The other angle for the proposing and tremendous support of Common Core
has been addressed via John Oliver and his HBO show "This Week Tonight". This
era of change has radically reformed the publishing market and one of the biggest areas of constant revenue is the educational marketplace. Once I saw his
telecast on this every assumption I had fell into place. Below is my theory – and
theory it is only on why this is happening. But Mr. Oliver pretty much nailed it.

Think about how a loss of paper textbooks has affected the textbook industry.
The same books are being sold but they are eBooks and for a much lower price.
So how does that affect the publisher if they are not printed therefore a cheaper
production price should allow for a cheap selling price – correct? Well yes if you
are living on a day to day budget and corporations don't do business that way.
They squirrel away profits – Apple's $170 Billion dollar cash reserve and usually
borrow to finance day to day operations. Now the interest rate on these loans is
predicated on profits. If profits are good you get a lower rate. If bad your rate
goes up. So if these corporations quickly go to a digital product and their
actually cash revenue stream doesn't match the anticipated profit amounts – in
real dollars –then their interest rate goes up and they will have huge trouble on
the balance sheet.

What does this have to do with Common Core? Well they are using the test
sales for Common Core to leverage the transition to a digital market. Basically
they have invented a need and are filling it in order to keep their balance sheets

in the black during the transition. So once again – in my humble opinion it appears that – paper is stopping the future of digital and in that future is contained the advancement of students.

Digital has a huge wake behind it and many boats won't survive.

Use of tablets

The use of tablets in K-12 has been spoken about on both sides of the issue. Educational companies like Amplify (Wireless Generation) now headed by Joel Klein ex-Chancellor of New York City school system has gone as far as bundling their applications on a tablet and provided this complete package as a solution.

Combines Innovative System for Digital Learning With More Rugged Device

> *(AUSTIN, Texas, March 3, 2014) Amplify today announced a collaboration with Intel Education to offer a more ruggedized tablet built for K-12 education. Available for the 2014-2015 school year, the new tablet features a durable industrial design that can withstand drops and spills; a break- and scratch-resistant screen made of Corning® Gorilla® Glass; an advanced Wi-Fi radio; and a tethered stylus. The new device is part of the Amplify Tablet System, which also includes instructional software, K-12 content and implementation support.*
>
> - *http://www.amplify.com/newsroom/press-release/amplify-intel*

This may not be the complete solution, but it's a serious investment by Amplify to augment their software by providing a hardware delivery platform that satisfies many needs basically a turn-key solution. There are some doubters and some believers, as you will see in the next two excerpts.

> *Universities are quaking at the thought of being replaced by tech upstarts. But few people think that under-16s can do without schools and teachers; it is just that new tools could help them do a better job. That may make them keener on ed-tech, and quicker to adopt it. Resistance is also being overcome by involving teachers in product design. Their fears that device-driven classes would curb spontaneity or cause pupils to ignore them prompted Amplify to include an override that lets them lock devices, so that pupils look up and listen.*

> *At $199 per pupil, per year, for tablet, set-up and software, Amplify looks pricey. But research by the Gates Foundation shows that spending on America's schools has more than doubled in the past four decades, with much of the extra money going on textbooks and updating computer hardware. Hand-held devices that can be customized look like a better deal. Investors are convinced: according to CB Insights, a consultancy, American ed-tech start-ups attracted $1.25 billion last year.*

http://www.economist.com/news/international/21603471-latest-innovations-promise-big-improvements-teaching-taking-learning-tablets

Now to review how these new devices – eReaders, tablets, iPads, etc. (which to me are nothing more than 21st century textbooks/backpacks) here are excerpts from digital technology actually being used in the classroom.

And Heather Blake, an Arlington second-grade teacher, was able to keep assignments flowing during the many snow days this past winter, sending daily messages with grammar lessons and math activities, directing home-bound students to measure the snow drifts or follow a recipe for snow ice cream.

"It's like we didn't really miss a beat," said Blake, who teaches at Jamestown Elementary School. "We just continued with our learning."…

"Computers can help students learn at their own pace, based on what they know rather than on whatever class they are in. Experts say this can be particularly helpful for a ninth-grader who reads at a fourth-grade level. Computers also have the potential to engage students through the same kinds of games, videos and social networks that captivate them during their free time."- http://www.washingtonpost.com/local/education/tablets-proliferate-in-nations-classrooms-and-take-a-swipe-at-the-status-quo/2014/05/17/faa27ba4-dbbd-11e3-8009-71de85b9c527_story.html

eTextbooks

Having been in educational publishing, when technology entered the arena I believe tremendously in the use of online textbooks - what is being called eTextbooks. Having watched my own children wear backpacks that looked like they were landing at Fallujah and seeing that some of those textbooks basically stopped at that time in history as well, I always believed that access to global, current, and multimedia content was the key to this new generation's ability to learn.

There have been good initiatives to bring this new archetype to fruition and commonality, but there has also been great hesitance. Some examples are below.

WHITE PLAINS, N.Y. — At Archbishop Stepinac High School, the back-packs got a whole lot lighter this year because nearly every book — from freshman biology to senior calculus — is now digital, accessible on students' laptops and tablets.

... History teacher Joe Cupertino says having so much "enrichment" available in the digital text means homework is productive and "frees us to do more discussion, more analysis in class."

Portanova says he's already seen academic improvement: The list of students on academic probation "has shrunk substantially, which I really attribute to this digital textbook library." -
http://www.nbcnews.com/business/business-news/ny-school-goes-all-digital-textbooks-f2D11792419

Gen-I

This is a term I came up with to combat the simplicity of the term "Millenials". The term "Millenials", to me, just has to do with a date or time and not an actual belief system. "Millenials" are just born at a certain time. It doesn't mean they live the life - it's just a date. Some actually purposedly go off the grid – embracing the 1960's commune-like mentality. And "Digital Natives" kind of means the same, but there could be a slightly different birth date. Gen-I means that they are "in-it-to-win-it" and "they can't help it". These young people are at the core of the movement because of both age and lifestyle combined. They're in school now, shaping how we teach by how they learn, and subsequently they'll be consuming and producing by those same patterns. They are the end-user we are designing the society for today.

In my humble opinion here is the definition of Gen-I.

Gen-i stands for generation interactive, isolated, iterative, Internet driven, immaterial, isogonics, isomorphic, (cyber) itinerant, inoculated, etc.
http://patrickaievoli.com/gen-ithe-rise-of-generation-interactive/

STEM & STEAM

Today there is great attention focused on not only using these new technologies, but *who* will be developing the future technologies. To many, it seems a step away from the liberal arts core of many colleges towards an almost vocational curriculum. To that point I argue that the combination of theory and application create a better good – at least in this point of history. My belief is that education should evolve to reflect and meet the needs of society. Today there is a focus on S.T.E.M.

A common definition of S.T.E.M.is the focus in education on

- Science

- Technology

- Engineering

- Math

A more in-depth definition might be as follows below.

> *STEM education is an interdisciplinary approach to learning where rigorous academic concepts are coupled with real-world lessons as students apply science, technology, engineering, and mathematics in contexts that make connections between school, community, work, and the global enterprise enabling the development of STEM literacy and with it the ability to compete in the new economy.* (Tsupros, 2009)

> - http://www.nsta.org/publications/news/story.aspx?id=59305

To include the study of art and design in STEM the Rhode Island School of Design (RISD) has helped in the following STEAM initiative- started by John Maeda.

> *STEAM is a movement championed by Rhode Island School of Design (RISD) and widely adopted by institutions, corporations and individuals.*

> *The objectives of the STEAM movement are to:*

> - *transform research policy to place Art + Design at the center of STEM*

> - *encourage integration of Art + Design in K–20 education*

> - *influence employers to hire artists and designers to drive innovation*

http://stemtosteam.org/

In my current position as a professor of design, and by using of technology to employ that design approach, I lean more towards STEAM than just STEM alone. However I do find it difficult to get behind an initiative that was born during Dr. Maeda's tenure at RISD when they purposely undercut his efforts to further lead that institution. Why would you as an institution advocate for such an initiative, but yet do everything you can to stop the progress of the individual who brought this to life and whom basically embodies this mindset? The only answer that comes to mind is a Machiavellian approach to education. *Don't actually do what you say... just make it look like you are doing this.* In my opinion, it's the basis for the demise of education and forwardly the demise of our country on the world stage. This approach harkens back to the political fight over Common Core. Don't actually support or denounce the initiative just be mindful of how your approach benefits your needs - bad to the bone – and at the core if you will.

MOOCs - Massive Open Online Courses

In my opinion, MOOCs are the major disruptor and solution in the world of education. They are literally giving away an Ivy League education for free, but the catch is – in many cases no credit and no degree. You can get both but that will cost you and rightly so – but the cost is dramatically lower than a traditional on-campus degree.

The first question that comes up when we speak of MOOCs is "what the hell is a MOOC?" Well here is a definition offered up by the New York Times.

> ### WHAT IS A MOOC ANYWAY?
>
> *Traditional online courses charge tuition, carry credit and limit enrollment to a few dozen to ensure interaction with instructors. The MOOC, on the other hand, is usually free, credit-less and, well, massive.*
>
> *...The evolving form knits together education, entertainment (think gaming) and social networking. Unlike its antecedent, open courseware — usually written materials or videotapes of lectures that make you feel as if you're spying on a class from the back of the room — the MOOC is a full course made with you in mind.*
>
> *The medium is still the lecture. Thanks to* <u>*Khan Academy*</u>*'s free archive of snappy instructional videos, MOOC makers have gotten the memo on the benefit of brevity: 8 to 12 minutes is typical. Then — this is key — videos pause perhaps twice for a quiz to make sure you understand the material or, in computer programming, to let you write code. Feedback is electronic. Teaching assistants may monitor discussion boards. There may be homework and a final exam.*
>
> - <u>http://www.nytimes.com/2012/11/04/education/edlife/massive-open-online-courses-are-multiplying-at-a-rapid-pace.html?pagewanted=all&_r=0</u>

And by massive, we mean massive. In some cases, over 150,000 students sign up for these classes with only a very small percentage finishing the course. So with anything this dramatic what are the reasons for such a shift? My belief is that the MOOC structure is nothing but a "loss leader" a sampling like COSTCO offers.

"Oh have you tired the barbeque chicken?" you know the trays that are passed around to entice the shopper to buy the whole chicken. Now, I am not saying these courses are of less quality but it isn't currently the whole chicken, but with the use of new technology they can be. They are the testing ground for a new model.

These MOOCs are being embraced by some of the most prestigious and largest colleges in the world. Below is a short list of some MOOC structures and the colleges and universities found at http://www.mooc.ca/providers.htm

MOOC and open Course Providers

Visit individual sites to view course lists.

- Alison Free courses in 10+ Course Categories."
- Apnacourse - course on PMP, ACP, CFP, CFA, FRM, ISTQB
- Canvas Network by Instructure
- Carnegie Mellon University Open Learning Initiative
- Class Central - Stanford, Coursera, MIT and Harvard led edX (MITx + Harvardx + BerkeleyX), and Udacity
- Coursera list of courses
- Curricki - open curriculua
- EdX courses
- FutureLearn, the Open University's MOOC branch
- iTunesU - some courses - guide from DIY University (Apple doesn't provide a list of courses, naturally); list of affiliates
- iversity - Berlin-based MOOC provider, listing courses in English
- Janux - the University of Oklahoma
- Miríada X - Spanish / Portugese courses
- MIT Open CourseWare (course materials only
- MOOC.fr - dédié à des MOOC francophones (premier MOOC, Internet : Tout Y est Pour Apprendre)
- NovoEd - a series of online classes from top institutions including Stanford GSB, Babson, and the Kauffman Foundation, with the majority free of charge.
- Open2Study (Australia)
- Open Education Europa, a Web site that aggregates MOOCs and other free online resources from European universities.
- Open HPI, Hasso Plattner Institute
- 信息技术在线互动课程的公开平台 OpenHPI Chinese-language MOOC portal.

- Open Learning courses

- Open Learn - Open University (UK), see menu at left

- P2P University - courses

- Qualt - Qualt advertises "Free mobile courses in internationally recognised professional qualifications. Anytime, anywhere." The courses are available for mobile devices only.

- SyMynd courses from NYU, University of Washington, McGill University

- Stanford's Free Online Courses

- Udacity courses

- Udemy list of online courses

- Universitat Politècnica de València - Spanish language

- University of the People - course catalogue

- Unow offers MOOCs in french (including this one reviewed here).

- WikiEducator content

- Wikiversity - 'schools'

- Open Yale courses

Arts reforms

In the art world there seems to be a reach back to the era of Abstract Expressionism - a style of art that I love and studied while in college. The form and surface of this style appeal to me personally and spiritually. It speaks to my soul, and is the best form of therapy I could ever undertake. The work of artists like deKooning, Diebenkorn, Gorky, Hartigan, Kline, Krasner, Pollock, Still, both excite and calm me in the same instance.

Today it seems this style is making a comeback. I have looked at the work of some current art students and see very similar styles in their work. *Why?* It seems like a harkening to go back to vinyl-like music. A desire to slow down and appreciate the humanity in the arts makes total sense. According to many of my colleagues in this field, "art is meant to be subversive" and this style could truly subvert the current direction of society. To bring the physical beauty of life back from the edge of virtual(ly) everything.

Even though earlier efforts and attempts to move in the direction of this new digital medium - with work from artists like Laurie Anderson, John Fekner, and Peter Gabriel - the desire for the physical seems to always come back to the forefront. My belief is that physical versus virtual has always rested back with art as a commodity. Great efforts... but at the end of the day, how do you sell this work and keep the art economy going forward? I understand the same is true for any form of large installation work or conceptual or performance, but there are many ways to document those efforts, and that becomes the commodity. But truly virtual? That's a problem. The move towards online and gif art is fun. It takes motion into the space but has a very Dadaesque feel to it. Like being ironic about technology and taking it as a joke while the grown-ups make sure everything works. This is all done as a show of repugnancy to the world of user technology while at the same time texting each other as to the newest place to get $5 coffee.

Physical versus virtual

This is a very big deal in the world of the arts, and especially in reference to the experience of viewing art, as in the showcase of a museum. Here is an excerpt from Art In America concerning that issue:

THE MUSEUM INTERFACE

by <u>Sarah Hromack</u>, <u>Rob Giampietro</u>

> "It's no longer a question of whether art institutions should have a virtual presence. Rather, the onus is being placed on designers to facilitate meaningful interactions with art that might occur in the gallery, via Web-based applications or in new hybrid spaces that merge the real and the virtual. Any attempt to augment an encounter with artwork using technological means invariably raises questions about the values we assign to certain modes of viewing. After all, isn't visiting a museum inherently tied to a very deep, very primary real-life experience? The promises and pitfalls of new

technologies are forcing museums to rebalance their traditional mandates to care for a collection of physical objects while enabling scholarship and providing the wider public an opportunity to engage with works of art. — R.G. and S.H. ...

Later in the same article after much discussion...

Yet, the future of museum visitor engagement will continue to mimic current technology trends: smartphones, "wearables" and proximity-based technologies such as the iBeacon. MoMA's most recent mobile application, Audio +, is a strong example of an institution recognizing a now—natural human behavior—in this case, the propensity of in—gallery photography—and designing for that behavior rather than sanctioning against it. Likewise, the soon-to-reopen Cooper Hewitt, Smithsonian Design Museum will proffer an interactive pen, co-designed with Hewlett-Packard, to each visitor who will in turn be permitted to "collect" objects throughout the institution by scanning museum labels, thereby "capturing" their visit to the museum for later access on a web address printed on their admission ticket. These digital experiments don't always work, and they certainly challenge still-held ideas about how people should and shouldn't behave in museums. But art institutions aren't churches, and the enthusiasm we see among visitors for bringing digital technology into the gallery suggests that we're witnessing a transformation in how the museum relates to its public. The assumptions and biases that will be overturned in that process remains another question entirely."

- *http://www.artinamericamagazine.com/news-features/magazine/the-museum-interface/*

The attempts and solutions discussed in this article seem promising and worthwhile. Only time will tell how and if they truly make an impact or are merely attempts to distract the viewer from the demise of the institution as a repository of value and taste.

Solutions have been attempted through many venues, both physical and virtual. One of the earliest attempts was "BitStreams" and the Whitney Artport. A 2001 article in New York magazine discusses the opening of this new effort.

"Digital artists are about to break down another boundary: the one between them and the art world's upper echelons. The Whitney's "BitStreams" exhibition, which opens March 22, is the first show devoted to such work at a major New York museum. Almost simultaneously, the San Francisco Museum of Modern Art has opened "010101: Art in Technological Times" -- an even broader survey of tech-influenced artwork. Downtown, a new media-arts umbrella organization called Eyebeam Atelier is raising $40 million for a new 90,000-square-foot art-and-technology museum set to come online, as it were, in Chelsea in 2004. And after several years of mainly watching from the sidelines, more New York galleries are showing -- and even selling -- digital work. "It's finally beginning seriously to infiltrate the

collector system," says Sandra Gering, a dealer who has been representing new-media artists since 1993...

For the Whitney, recent history has raised the stakes somewhat. Its former director David Ross is widely recognized as a tech-art visionary, having made his reputation with early and vociferous support of both video and Internet art. He left his Madison Avenue perch in 1998 to head sfmoma, taking Intel, which spent $6 million sponsoring Ross's two-part blockbuster "American Century" show, along with him..."

http://nymag.com/nymetro/arts/features/4507/

Museums and online work

Extraordinary cultural icons such as the Guggenheim, Whitney, and MOMA have and had, for a certain length of time, invested deeply into the online space. With such entities as YouTube Play, Whitney Artport, and MOMA online a true effort into understanding this new space has been made since the early days of the web. It's a very difficult space to evaluate and curate since the nature of the space ebbs and flows so erratically – just like the nature of the subject matter.

The one venue that stood the test of time, and seems to constantly be reinventing itself, is the Whitney Artport. A quick description from the site is listed below.

"Artport is the Whitney Museum's portal to Internet art and an online gallery space for commissions of net art and new media art. Originally launched in 2002, Artport provides access to original art works commissioned specifically for artport by the Whitney; documentation of net art and new media art exhibitions at the Whitney; and new media art in the Museum's collection." http://whitney.org/Exhibitions/Artport

I personally love how Artport archives the attempts from the past years, beginning with the 2002 Biennale. To be able to still view that work, sometimes feels like visiting an abandoned amusement park or like Atlantis' ruins – an old friend typically says. It is a good thing, but at times feels pretty melancholic.

Work like "People's Portrait" is similar to Instagram or Tumblr before they even existed. Twitter is equivalent to the work of Duchamp and Ray Johnson after they existed.

Guggenheim - YouTube Play - http://youtu.be/NDv4oPpj8vs

This incarnation of combining the artist and the public was an amazing and gorgeous culmination of so many forms of art and diverse thesis concepts. Yes, it was video art, but the levels of thought in each piece was not just merely video. In my opinion, the video was just capturing the thought process and the installation was just amazing from the outside of the building compared to the inside use of Wright's architecture.

Description from the Guggenheim site:

> *YouTube Play focused on the most exceptional talent working in the ever-expanding realm of online video. Developed by YouTube and the Guggenheim Museum in collaboration with HP, YouTube Play attracted innovative, original, and surprising videos from around the world, regardless of genre, technique, background, or budget.*

> **Guggenheim Exhibition**
> *On view at the Guggenheim Museums in New York, Bilbao, Berlin, and Venice from October 22 to 24, 2010, the top 25 videos made up the ultimate YouTube playlist: a selection of the most unique, innovative, groundbreaking video work being created and distributed online during the past two years. The videos and artists were celebrated at an event at the Guggenheim Museum in New York on October 21, which was livestreamed to a worldwide audience at youtube.com/play.*

THE JURY

Laurie Anderson

Animal Collective, featuring Deakin (Josh Dibb), Geologist (Brian Weitz), and Panda Bear (Noah Lennox)

Darren Aronofsky

Douglas Gordon

Ryan McGinley

Marilyn Minter

Takashi Murakami

Shirin Neshat

Stefan Sagmeister

Apichatpong Weerasethakul

Nancy Spector, Jury Chair

- http://www.guggenheim.org/new-york/online/participate/youtube-play

Summary

So in the end what is the solution? How do we combine the original conceptual work of Duchamp with the endless possibilities of digital? Well hell if I know but I personally believe that the work of artists like Camille Utterback and Daniel Rozin are some inspiring versions of crossing that bridge between physical and virtual. Please visit their sites and see the work. They don't need my help but just like to share.

Chapter 7 - The real disruptors

This time they're real, and this time they're pissed.

So far, this book has concentrated on design and digital disruptors – not really tangible solutions. In this chapter I would like to introduce the real physical ones. Some of them have been mentioned here before, but for the most part this chapter talks about the actual physical and manufacturing products that have undergone some massive reformations.

<u>Physical and manufactured disruptions</u>

To me, the fist name that should be on this list is Elon Musk part of the self-named PayPal mafia. He seems like a modern-day Henry Ford and Thomas Edison combined. His work in the fields of space travel exploration (SpaceX), electric cars (Tesla Motors and Hydro Loop) is fascinating. Just think about what these current inventions will disrupt - reusable rockets that don't cost a gazillion dollars – electric cars and the oil industry - travelling between cities at record speeds for minimal cost? This is the work of Nikola Tesla brought to life again through Elon Musk.

Quick Bio –

> *Elon Musk was born in South Africa and became a multimillionaire in his late twenties when he sold his start-up company, Zip2, to a division of Compaq Computers. He went on to more early success launching PayPal via a 2000 merger, Space Exploration Technologies Corp. (SpaceX) in 2002, and Tesla Motors in 2003. Musk made headlines in May 2012 when SpaceX launched a rocket that would send the first commercial vehicle to the International Space Station. - http://www.biography.com/people/elon-musk-20837159*

Here is also a list of the other top 50 Disruptors for 2014 from CNBC website.

SpaceX	company that wants to send you to space and colonize Mars.
Warby Parker	Taking on the Luxottica eyewear machine.
Etsy	A big voice for small artisans.
Motif Investing	Building theme-based portfolios online.
Palantir Technologies	Silicon Valley's CIA operative.
GitHub	Cracking the code on collaboration.
Aereo	The company TV hopes will die.
Moderna Therapeutics	Reprogramming cells to fight disease.
Spotify	The most controversial act in music.
Uber	The 21st-century taxi service.
Zuora	A renewal in the subscription business model.
ChargePoint	Putting the gas station out of business.
Dataminr	The search for intelligence on Twitter.
Skybox Imaging	The spy who came into the Google fold.
Stripe	The start-up challenging PayPal.
TransferWise	Getting bankers out of the forex biz.
Personal Capital	A 360-degree view of your finances.
Quirky	Crowdsourcing an idea for basement tinkerers.
Pure Storage	Predicting a flash flood of data.
Wealthfront	Silicon Valley's plan to oust wealth managers.
Fullscreen	YouTube's hot multichannel talent network.
EcoMotors	Turning the engine inside out, in Detroit's backyard.
Shape Security	Putting organized cybercrime out of biz.
Dropbox	The 800-pound gorilla in the cloud IPO room.
Cool Planet Energy Systems	From farm to fuel, and back to farm.
AngelList	Getting disruptors the money they need to disrupt.
BrightRoll	Betting detergent ads on TV won't wash.
Yext	Resurrecting the Yellow Pages.
DocuSign	Sign on the dotted e-line.
Apptio	A cloud-based Peter Drucker.
Nebula	A private cloud the size of a pizza box.
Pinterest	The world's bulletin board.
Lending Club	Borrowing without banks.
Redfin	The only real estate broker who hates commissions.

Coinbase	The closest thing bitcoin has to a central bank.
Hampton Creek Foods	The egg comes first; no chicken necessary.
Bill.com	Making sure the check's never in the mail again.
Rent The Runway	Nice dress. Can I borrow it?
Nexmo	How billion-dollar start-ups text.
Fon	The Airbnb meets Uber and Aereo of Wi-Fi.
Airbnb	The newest idea in room service: renting one.
MongoDB	Solving humongous data problems.
Oscar	Health insurance for the Obamacare era.
Kumu Networks	A much-needed boost for wireless networks.
Betterment	Robo-advising for the masses.
Kymeta	Bill Gates' next potential blockbuster.
Twilio	Riding the mobile-app wave.
Snapchat	The app for selfie photo lovers.
Kickstarter	Cashing in from the crowd.
Birchbox	Free samples, for a price.

- http://www.cnbc.com/id/101734664

But obviously, since that's an entire book or set of encyclopedias, I'll choose one that I foresee having a huge impact, and is a combination of physical and digital - 3D printing. Ah yes, still printing... but definitely different. The technology is relatively old now, like 33 years old, but I think it will have an impact that spreads throughout many industries and affects many jobs.

Quick History of 3D printing

According to the website redorbit.com, the history of 3D printing goes back to 1982 and to two individuals named Hideo Kodama and Charles Hull.

> *"The first published account of a printed solid model was made by Hideo Kodama of Nagoya Municipal Industrial Research Institute in 1982. The first working 3D printer was created in 1984 by Charles W. Hull of 3D Systems Corp. Hull published a number of patents on the concept of 3D printing, many of which are used in today's additive manufacturing processes. Of course, 3D printing in the early days was very expensive and not feasible for the general market. As we moved into the 21st century, however, costs drastically dropped, allowing 3D printers to find their way to a more affordable market.*
>
> *The cost of 3D printers has even decreased in the years from 2010 to 2013, with machines generally ranging in price from $20,000 just three*

years ago, to less than $1,000 in the current market. Some printers are even being developed for under $500, making the technology increasingly avail-able to the average consumer."

Read more at http://www.redorbit.com/education/reference_library/general-2/history-of/1112953506/the-history-of-3d-printing/#wz983px6VlLE75hz.99

Why do I find this to be a disruptor? Well, think of all the things that can now be printed in 3D, and how these items are going to affect their respective indus-tries. Then, think of all the people who work in factories and plants listed below, and all the products they manufacture.

Here's a short list:

> Aerospace
>
> Aerospace parts
>
> Architecture
>
> Automotive design
>
> Car parts
>
> Construction
>
> Dental and medical technology
>
> Engineering
>
> Eyewear
>
> Fashion
>
> Food
>
> Footwear
>
> Human organs
>
> Human prosthetics
>
> Industrial design
>
> Jewelry
>
> Military
>
> Small manufactured items
>
> Weapons

http://www.redorbit.com/education/reference_library/general-2/history-of/1112953506/the-history-of-3d-printing/#wz983px6VlLE75hz.99

Imagine you're in space and a part broke. It could be small and simple, but it's necessary to complete the mission. What could you do? Would you send another space ship to bring the spare part to the space station? Or, if the space station had a 3D printer onboard… voila! The part appears! Read about how this recently happened.

"Space Station's 3D Printer Makes Wrench From 'Beamed Up' Design -

The 3D printer aboard the International Space Station has wrapped up the first phase of its orbital test run by cranking out a ratchet wrench whose design was beamed up from Earth.

The wrench, along with the 19 other objects built by the orbiting <u>3D printer</u> thus far, will travel to Earth early next year, where engineers will compare the objects with ground samples produced by the same machine before it launched, NASA officials said.

"We can't wait to get these objects home and put them through structural and mechanical testing," Quincy Bean, of NASA's Marshall Space Flight Center in Huntsville, Alabama, said in a statement. "We really won't know how well this process worked in space until we inspect the parts and complete these tests." <u>http://www.space.com/28095-3d-printer-space-station-ratchet-wrench.html</u>

Now let's bring that idea down to Earth. You have a water bottle top that your child needs for soccer practice or that you need for the office. You swear you brought it home, but you can't find it. You have to get to work so there isn't any time to stop and buy another. So, while you take your shower, your 3D printer "prints" the new bottle top using the plans you just downloaded. Usually within 5 to 10 minutes the job is done and at a fraction of the cost. While that may be great for you, it's not for the person who works at the manufacturing plant and needs that top to get lost or go missing in order to keep demand up – and keep their job.

Chapter 8 – The New Design

In this chapter we will discuss a version of this new design world – interaction design. Interaction design is comprised of two main components – UX user experience and UI user interface design.

Examples and ratings of UX Design jobs from numerous sources here:

money.cnn.com/best jobs

14. User Exp. Designer

Brooklyn-based freelance user experience designer Louisa Armbrust

Median pay: $89,300

Top pay: $138,000

10-year job growth: 18%

A user experience designer spends a lot of the day thinking about how a person interacts with digital products, like websites. It might be about rearranging buttons on a webpage, or changing the way someone interacts with an online educational tool.

What's great: These designers are responsible for raising the bar when it comes to experiencing digital products. That skill is increasingly in demand. "User experience has caught on so much, both as something that people enjoy doing and something that is more and more widely recognized as being valuable to a growing number of companies," said user experience designer Louisa Armbrust. --J.E.

Quality of life ratings:
Personal satisfaction: B | Benefit to society: B | Telecommuting: A | Low stress: A

http://money.cnn.com/gallery/pf/2015/01/27/best-jobs-2015/14.html

U.S. News - Job Profile –Web Developer (UX Designer)

Overall Score (3.8 out of 5)
Number of Jobs 28,500
Median Salary $63,160
Unemployment Rate 3.8 percent

This Job is Ranked in

Best Technology Jobs	#**4**
Best STEM Jobs	#**4**
The 100 Best Jobs	#**11**

Although some Web developers will design a website's front and back end, many Web development companies split these responsibilities. For instance, some Web developers will work in Photoshop to create the overall design, while others will be in charge of writing the code in programming languages such as HTML and CSS. Developers must take into account a client's products or services as well as the target market to create a site that appeals to the client's customers or intended audience. The job requires a knowledge of software programs, Web applications and programming languages such as the aforementioned HTML and CSS, as well as a solid understanding of design principles. Work environments for Web developers vary from large corporations or governments to small businesses. Developers may be full-time employees, part-time consultants or work on a contract basis as freelancers.

The Bureau of Labor Statistics projects about 20 percent employment growth for Web developers by 2022. During that period, about 28,500 new jobs will need to be filled in an industry that already has roughly 141,400 positions. The expansion of e-commerce is expected to be the main driver of Web developer job growth in the next decade. As more companies offer or expand their online retail presence, more Web developers will be needed to build the websites visited by consumers to purchase their favorite products. Increased reliance on mobile search is another reason the industry's employment growth should remain strong. ...

Salary

The BLS reports that Web developers made a median salary of $63,160 in 2013. The highest-paid in the profession earned $110,350, while the lowest-paid earned $33,320 that year. Computer systems design and information services employ the largest share of Web developers in the field. The highest-paid positions can be found in the metropolitan areas of San Jose, California; San Francisco; and Baltimore.

Salary Range

75th Percentile	**$85,270**
Median	**$63,160**
25th Percentile	**$44,550**

- See Full Salary Data

- See Web Developer Jobs Near You

Training

Some employers prefer a bachelor's degree in a computer-related field such as computer science or information technology. Web developers may also get certifications, including Certified Web Developer, Certified Internet Webmaster, Advanced Web Developer and in Mobile Application Development, all of which demonstrate varying levels of expertise. But other employers put more weight on a prospective employee's previous work. "Focus on the portfolio," Ruditser says. "Even if you don't have real world experience, you can make up your own mock projects. It's not about being polished; it's about being creative."

http://money.usnews.com/careers/best-jobs/web-developer

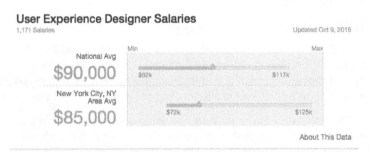

http://www.glassdoor.com/Salaries/user-experience-designer-salary-SRCH_KO0,24.htm

UX – defining the user experience

UX is basically aesthetic and the function combined into one working proto-type. This process involves a diverse series of skill sets. A typical UX designer needs to have a true sense of visual design – typography, image, color theory and all of the basic elements and principles of traditional design. Now add to this mix the ability to understand how programming works and how the user prefers things to work. A great add on from the world of liberal arts would be some study or possibly a minor in sociology, psychology and anthropology. How do humans' like to interact with objects? What are our patterns? What are our typical likes and dislikes? How do we go about interacting?

The process of UX design usually starts with a meeting to discuss goals and objectives. From then on a study and research is conducted to establish priori-ties and determine the stakeholders and the end user. Once these goals have been established a series of design audits take place usually dealing with the "what", "where" and "why" of the project.

"What" is the project going to be used for?

"What" needs to be contained within the project?

"Where" will it be situated?

"Why" is that the best practice?

Once these benchmarks have been established wireframes of the page divi-sion starts. Wireframes are typically done with just simple boxes or shapes establishing "real estate" on the screen. This is usually followed by image, typo-graphical and color theory choices. All of this is driven by the actually content (image and text or database) of the project. After this process has been achieved and reviewed actual minor interactivity is implemented to test flow of content and user choices. This process is repeated and iterated numerous times over the course of the project.

From this quick and simple paragraph one can easily see this isn't your granddaddy's graphic design world anymore. And this is where the big names start stepping into the picture.

Notable UX Designers

A leading designer in this area today is the aforementioned David Kelley. His work has been heralded for decades from his early days working with Steve Jobs to recent iterations at IDEO and dschool at Stanford. We have talked about Mr. Kelley at length but let's hear what he has to say about the UX process.

> *"The designer… has a passion for doing something that fits somebody's needs, but that is not just a simple fix. The designer has a dream that goes beyond what exists, rather than fixing what exists… the designer wants to create a solution that fits in a deeper situational or social sense." – David Kelley, Founder of IDEO, in Bringing Design to Software by Terry Winograd*

"As far as the customer is concerned, the interface is the product." — *Jef Raskin*

The one thing all these viewpoints share is the concept of preparation and planning. It seems to me and I have witnessed through my three decades of teaching that designers especially the young ones don't enjoy the planning stage they want to jump in and keep pushing pixels around until they see something they like. Try to put that time on a billable client sheet!

And from high upon Olympus...

"Design is not just what it looks like and feels like. Design is how it works." - *Steve Jobs*

The UX process in greater detail

According to many sources and as has been stated before the UX process is all about research and preparation. Visual design is a given and the use of traditional design elements and principles are the tool set from where everything is based however the planning and preparation stages are where these tools work either effectively or not.

Maintaining the Brand presence

One area that makes the transition is marketing the brand. To me the biggest piece of the puzzle is how to integrate the brand presence into every stage of the user experience. How do you keep the metaphor going for a user experience project? What do you use?

One of my students has integrated the material used in the car that the app is for along with good placement of the logo. My suggestion would be to make the buttons on the app look like the cars buttons and latches - Integrate, integrate, integrate! The user should always feel like they are in the environment that the app or site is presenting.

Another area of great concern with brand presence is color and typography. The entire experience must reflect the brand's use of these elements. Also not to speak of the principles espoused by the brand. Examples would be the difference between an app for Ikea and an app for Overstock.com Ikea should be light and airy and very clean and concise like the product line. Where Overstock.com should kind of look like its name. Full of imagery and choices but like Steve says it needs to actually work so form should never trump function. There needs to be a proper balance to evoke the correct brand presence while satisfying the user's needs.

If all of this sound like advertising or marketing well quite frankly it is just that. Every time you use a product or service you need to remember that feeling and associate it with that brand. Just like any product – if you wear Nike you know they are Nike – not just the logo but, the quality of the shoe. If you use an Apple product you know it's an Apple product.

UX Process step by step

According to an article in Smashingmagazine.com – the process in its early stages goes in this order.

- **The research phase** is where you immerse yourself in the project to get the background you'll need to make design decisions later in the project. During this phase you will try to learn as much about your client's business, objectives, users and competitors as possible.

- **The design phase** is where you work out how what you are designing will work and how it will fit together. This phase will define its scope, its features and functionality and how it behaves.

- **The validation phase** is where you identify whether what you came up with in the design phase actually works with its intended audience. This phase is typically followed by further rounds of design and testing to solve the problems you inevitably find when you test with users.

http://www.smashingmagazine.com/2013/01/effectively-planning-ux-design-projects/

As Antonelli has stated in video interviews and in writing that design will evolve into theoretical and applied areas. Slowly the lines between science and visual will blur and a good part of the development process of a project will be based on analytics and prior structures.

As you can see below the table lists all stages of a user centered design project, basically interaction design and the UX portion of the project. It is almost clinical in nature.

Smashingmagazine.com – "Planning UX Design"

USER-CENTERED REDESIGN PROJECT OUTLINE

Constraints: Huge complexity, high-profile project but good budget and excellent client buy-in for a UX approach.

UX Activity	Timing
Kick-off meeting	1 day
Desk research and document review	2 days
User research	10 days
Stakeholder interviews	3 days
Presentation of findings to board	1 day
Stakeholder interviews	3 days
Prototype development	10 days
Validation testing	5 days
Wireframes, stakeholder interviews and amends	10 days
Validation testing	5 days
Wireframe amends	2 days
Handover to visual design and development	0.5 days
Sign-off workshops	2 days
Post live usability review	10 days

Editor's Note: We are delighted to share this chapter on "Planning UX Projects" which was taken from the book "Smashing UX Design : Foundations for Designing Online User Experiences."

Full disclosure - this table is extremely similar to the process I use with my graduate students. Of course they do not believe it is used or a necessity. This book is for them as much as anyone.

Moving towards a "profession"

With all of this information and structure you can start to see how much the design industry has evolved into one of the "professions". For years, designers were thought of as a vocational – handcraft group. Where your ability to advance in this field was based on how well you could use the tools. The actual physical tools – ruling pens, Exacto knives, tweezers, etc. - like a high-end auto mechanic. Rarely was a designer thought of as someone who worked with their brain not their hands.

The process is simple and straight forward - the key part that generates confusion is iteration - the constant repeating of the process with slight changes – but very critical changes.

To that end most of the time on the project can be spent on analyzing and developing the "why" as well as the "what" and "how" components of UX. Using market analysis as a guide the team starts from that analysis to determine the goals of the project and build from there with the typical steps of the project process - design audits, wireframes, digital assets, prototyping and iterations.

After this process is complete usually the team then starts the actual build of the project incorporating and then iterating from analytics and trends. As with any project end viability is one of the main concerns.

Once the project has been developed the team has a presentation event, which includes a written document, short concise deck presentation and the actual working prototype.

Lots of work goes into making sure you can order that *"Half-DeCaf-HalfCaf-PumpkinSpice-Latte-Vente"* while you are on your way to meet your friends.

And here is a recent article in Kiplinger.com describing the future of this field and how current traditional analogue designers could make the transition.

Worst College Majors for Your Career 2015-2016

10. Graphic Design

*Studying graphic design doesn't lay out a great-looking career path, but looks can be deceiving. **Graphic designers specializing in print—working at newspapers, magazines and other publishers, for example—are facing major cutbacks along with the rest of the industry.** On the other hand, people focused on creating designs and images for mobile devices, Web sites and the like are in higher demand as all sorts of businesses look to develop and improve* *their digital presence. So if your heart is set on graphic design, skew your studies toward a technology-centric career path.*

Alternate major

*Better yet, try majoring in **multimedia and Web design** instead. The median salary for these degree holders starts at $43,400 a year and moves up to $59,500 by mid-career. With either major, you can land a job as a Web developer, in a field that is expected to add 23.5% more new positions by 2024. The typical pay is about $57,700 a year—better than the $42,600 earned by most graphic designers. Plus, it gives you plenty of opportunities to break into the hot tech sector and perhaps gain the work experience needed to become a highly paid and sought-after software developer (among our best jobs for the future). Read more at http://www.kiplinger.com/slideshow/college/T012-S001-worst-college-majors-for-your-career-2015-2016/index.html#3TKYLolB4ms2mCZ2.99*

Analogue to digital again

Now as the world goes from analogue to digital some still consider themselves "pixel pushers" not "concept pushers". Analogue designers are having issue here – the process eludes them. In my opinion and through my experience teaching groups of students you can see who - "gets it" and who - "doesn't get it". I joke with them that they just want to do nice drawings and put them on the refrigerator at home.

The next group that makes the conversion is the "creative" types - the ones that come up with good concepts and sort of strange solutions. They start to move in the right direction but then get stuck and can't get past the simple ten screen projects. As the projects get more complex they lose interest or can't seem to realize the importance of finishing.

Another group that gets it and sees their place in this new venue are the "truly creative". The ones who can maybe write the concept out and see it but may have not studied the software or may not have the completely analytical brain to make the next steps possible. Their advantage is that they see the pieces in the distance and no how to make them work together. As they now popular saying goes "I play the orchestra". They recognize the skills needed enlist and motivate those individuals and always keep focus on project goals and brand presence. They can place the pieces of the puzzle in line. They can usually also see the variations and the "what ifs"? This group sees the future and realizes their role in that future.

Analogue has dropped to second place and digital now has taken the lead. How we design for that transition is the basis of the new design frontier and in my opinion where the future lies for most of us designers – young and old.

Chapter 9 - Surfing those Waves

Being Digital – Again.

In conclusion of this work there are still many questions left to answer. However, I don't propose to have those answers, just a strong hunch of the future direction, given my experience and the conditions we're witnessing. Let me explain with an analogy. Many people think of the "surfer dude" as an airhead. Just somebody who hangs around and dreams of that big chance – gnarly! A friend once explained to me what actually goes into surfing and surviving on a piece of Styrofoam out in the middle of the ocean. It easily could look like the surfer is wasting time walking the beach, just staring out at the ocean. In reality, they're trying to figure out what the waves are doing that day, and before they go out on that board, they take the time to look around contemplating all the angles. They don't know which direction the wave will actually break, but they have an idea based on their experience and on what the ocean is doing that day.

In order not to leave the reader hanging, I wanted to practice what I preach. I reached out on Facebook to some old students who are now practicing teachers, designers, and developers to get their opinion about what needs to be done in this new Digital Incunabula. This small cohort represents positions in advertising agencies, digital marketing firms, retailers, and K-12 teaching. Below are their responses from those questions taken directly from those Facebook posts. Afterall, surfing is surfing, no matter where you do it!

Where should the focus be placed within education during this age of technology – theory or technology?

MB - In my opinion, you need to have great skills using the tools of the trade, but the theory makes a big difference if you want to be a great designer and sell your services... At the end, if you are not able to sell yourself or your services, you will struggle in this business... Therefore, I would focus on theory, art theory.

DJRV - Theory. Software constantly changes and designers need to be able to speak fluently agnostic of their applications. The most common problem we face in the industry today are with designers who cannot communicate effectively, both to their colleagues and clients.

Patrick Aievoli - so far so good - DJRV and MB and from two tech oriented designers - actually very good but here's my bigger question. If you have time - be a little more specific... like Information architecture - UX and IX, and how about some sociology and digital anthropology?

JLBH - Theory... Information Architecture and the psychology of design combined can be more powerful than learning a software technology that changes every year, or sooner. If you have a strong foundation on which to make intelligent design (visual and usability) decisions, the tools can be learned and mastered.

AP - Theory. Software is a tool. People might say software because everyone wants to know every tool out there nowadays. But you can fail at using the tools if you don't have the theory. Learn the rules before you try breaking them.

JG - I agree with the above. What separates a real designer from a knockoff "$99 Logos" joint is that a designer understands aesthetics and can tap into their knowledge and experience to give a client's idea a vision. Anyone can learn software but without the underlying knowledge of composition and design aesthetics, it looks like a club flyer.

SOR - Software. Unless you are the next design god, you are being told what to do by a certain deadline by people who think they know what they are talking about. Know your stuff. Be able to create above and beyond your task and always impress and improve your skills along the way. Creativity doesn't always pay the bills.

So far, the tech people say theory and the theory people say software. It seems like a balance between the both so here's the next question... Which is easier? Learning how to interpret theory into quality design, or learning software? in other words, can you learn quality problem solving as easily as you can learn software?

JG - Hmm good question with a lot of variables. I think a lot of it depends on the learning style of the student...but on the whole...I'd say a lot more understand skills than they know how to take their project to the next level. Especially when it comes to being able to integrate the software as a means of conducting what they want to get their idea across. I think time is a variable too. They may not "get" it now but who's to say they won't later? Answer doesn't have an absolute.

MB - In my opinion, it is easier to learn (a) software than become a quality problem solving expert... But, I believe that we need to place another variable on the problem solving factor, which would be Nurture.

JG - Good call. Effectiveness and nurture of the instructor. Lots of confidence building.

Patrick Aievoli - "a lot more understand skills than they know how to take their project to the next level." yep polite way of saying production over creative

JG - Yup. It's a level 1 class though. Once they get the meat, when they get to level 2, I get to work on more concept development with them. Often those who take the more advanced class are more motivated as a possible career choice vs. someone just taking an elective to try it out.

AP - Sorry the programmer in me likes problem solving. This theory trumps software. When you're in the field, you see a lot of people claiming they know the software but they really don't.

Patrick Aievoli - AP – So, you are saying what you can do with the software is bigger than how to use the software?

AP - Yes, that's exactly my point. Example, if you can write solid html or css, you can write it in any program you want. Most people don't know that you can write in a text editor and it'll work. Software is just another tool. An extension of your hand. Theory is all your mind and that should be limitless. The people who pick software are production focused and like to stay current. The theorists are those who invent the software or application. Oh, I can keep going lol! Go watch the movie Limitless.

Patrick Aievoli - "The theorists are those who invent the software or application" or how to put together the pieces to solve the problem and subsequently push towards a new structure?

AP - That's pretty much my point.

AP - Lol I'll put it dollar value, software = 65k - 80k a year. Theorists 120k - 180k (probably more but I rest my case lol)

Patrick Aievoli - Yep and software goes down with outsourcing - theorists get percentage of sales.

EDJ - BB'rs always make more money. Theories are just that. Theories... Some are based on fact but that doesn't mean any theory is true. Most of it is opinion. If you're smart and good at bS'ng then you can claim yourself to be a theorist. People did not believe Einstein was for real until his famous theories were made factual.

If you want to make a lot of money you don't become a designer or a theorist. You become the salesperson that sells the designs or ideas. Or if you happen to be a designer with sales, BS'ng skills and a business sense, then you can make a lot of money.

Software programmers are not artists. They happen to be very knowledgeable about binary language and true and false statements. Is language considered a design or a form of communication? I don't believe a binary function to be a design. It is 0's and 1's arranged, programmed or "developed" to perform a specific function. If it is not arranged in an exact manner you will get a friendly pop up that is "designed" to remind you that something is not making sense.

The question was how design should be taught.

First talk about what it is. What constitutes design? How does it differ from art? Are they the same? No... Why? etc...

I'm a graphic designer by trade, but do I consider myself an artist? No. I'm not an artist because I can't do whatever I want using whatever medium at my disposal and have fun watching people decide whether it's art or not.

I'm a designer because I take information and arrange it logically to make sense visually in order to clearly communicate a message. Could I claim myself to be an information architect? Theoretically, yes. I could sell it...

Design theory was developed so people could be taught how to be an artist or designer. True artists are those people who are creatively gifted and resourceful. They are passionate about their work and use anything and everything at their disposal. Graphic Designers are visual problem solvers and are extremely limited when it comes to creative license. They have to color inside the lines of clarity and specificity in order to be functional.

Are the ancient cave drawings works of art or an example of design? What was the purpose, how was it fulfilled? Was the intent to tell a story or show others how to draw animals and people the right way? The arrangement of the characters and how they relate to each other is how the story is communicated the design is how the forms of the figures were depicted. They were not just stick figures. There were no theorists telling them how to draw a horse or a person the right way.

I'm sure there were critics though, just watch "History of the World Part 1"

Patrick Aievoli - "What was the purpose" according to Meggs and Heller they were drawn to practice the hunt - small chips and broken arrowheads found at base...

AD - I agree, the technical aspects of design is practiced so much more than the theoretical part of it, I would like more theory. What makes a great ad, and why?

Patrick Aievoli - "Designers are visual problem solvers and are extremely limited when it comes to creative license." This is true on Long Island, but not in NYC with the campaigns like "I shipped my pants" FCBDraft – It matters where you are working.

EDJ   - Yes, definitely matters where you are working, the type of designer you are, and what the purpose of your project is.... And budget of course!

JR - As comprehensive a curricula as possible- both theory AND technique emphasized, or these days theory AND software. The why is subjective on both the institutional level, and varies from student to student on an individual subjective level- the obligation for the student is to both have their own "why" and ask the various institutions they are considering applying to "why"- then the student, and parents as well in many instances, must see if the series of "whys" overlap, and which institutions best overlap with the "why" from every party. Student why, Institution why, Parent why, and then a job market which doesn't care why as much as how, or maybe they have a why which changes every 10 minutes. My best answer is just as balanced and as broad a curriculum as possible, as having the widest knowledge base and widest skill set as possible (simultaneously) will best serve the student these days- when more is required than ever from employers or freelance clients alike.

RG - I so want to answer this question but I'm too tired after a 14 hr straight session of ideation and concept development for an experiential event logistics company. No theory just hard free association based on methodically crafted brand positioning. Starting with sketches! In pencil! On paper!!!

JLBH - Remember, everyone thinks they're a "designer" because they can "create" using software. Knowing the software is also crucial- to bring a design to life. There's a strong balance- but remember, without design knowledge/theory (NOT art history per say), knowing the software won't be important enough to succeed (at least in the design sense). A strong balance! Based on the comments in this conversation, Facebook suggested this article. I skimmed so far, but here goes: http://artbackwash.blogspot.com/.../dont-be-tooler.html...

"You can lead a designer to a computer, but you can't make them draw."

Patrick Aievoli - I kind of just realized - I think I held my first distance learning class on Facebook??? - I would have used LinkedIn but nobody actually talks there?

Patrick Aievoli   - RG - very funny - *"session of ideation and concept development for an experiential event logistics company. No theory just hard free association based on methodically crafted brand positioning. Starting with sketches! In pencil! On paper!!!"*

You all know I have lived software but now today stuff has shifted. Software skills are a given - so it's "Back to the Future IV"???

Why are the teachers not moving forward to teach the "why" since most of this new Generation knows software so much better than the last group 10 years ago?

LM - Because the group doing the teaching is from the early eras of design through tech - they had to struggle to get over the hump of learning to use the tech. The way they learned colors the way they teach just as much as math and history and language teachers' methods are colored by the way they learned their subjects. Theory was secondary because keeping up with the changing technologies had to come first to be competitive - anything they needed to know about good design could be learned by looking around them and trusting that their gut was being informed by the examples they saw in practice. The only reason we've shifted to you needing to ask why theory is such a secondary topic is because of how much more accessible tech is to the current generations- and how that's caused an over abundance of people who think they can design because they can work the software even though they have little artistic intuition.

Patrick Aievoli - LM, good answer. But why don't the teachers switch? Many schools today focus on the tech not the theory and tech combined? High Schools are doing a great job prepping them with software - so now is it college's turn to run forward?

LM - Where are you going to find the teachers who still know the theory and can translate it for this generation? Even in film school I was taught theory by osmosis. Which only works if you can put blinders on to all the junk. And the theory of what makes good design seems to shift with cultural shifts in style - the design of the US of the 50s doesn't fully translate to what is considered good design today - in large part because of the very technology that caused the shift away from teaching theory. That actually goes for all the art forms in which I've dabbled. There are always things that resonate forever, but the bulk of design has changed. Before anyone can try to teach design theory again, someone needs to figure out what it really is. Is there enough that's permanent to really teach it? Or was theory really just a reflection of the commonly accepted styles of the time?

DJRV - Tech is irrelevant unless you're a developer. If you're a designer, tech is valuable; however, 90% of interviewers are looking for conceptual, fluent and marketable ideation. Inherently, a good designer well understands their tech and by virtue of their profession seeks to master those platforms—much like a painter and his brush. It's the teacher's job to encourage a never-ending reach to use the most efficient tools; however, its most beneficial if the teacher grows their students theoretical and historical understanding. At the end of the day, designers who get hired have experience, or the technical/theoretical ability to make up for the lack thereof. Not the Photoshop wizards who can make water droplets in 30 seconds. That's production art, and that too is mostly theoretical understanding of press/digital/web production.

LM - Designers very much had to change in response to tech. Not only did their medium change but, all the tools which they have access to. Developers are creating the tech and in the case of web implementing the designers' vision - designers are utilizing that tech to actualize their designs. And having to design for interactive functionality, responsive sites, etc is very, very different from needing to create a single panel billboard or magazine ad. Those still occur but are typically integrated into a tech-centric campaign.

EDJ - It's hard for teachers to teach "why" they are being phased out of a job. They know most of the students nowadays are extremely tech savvy and can utilize the Internet and various social outlets to learn about what they want to specialize in. Teachers need to keep up with technology. If they don't their expertise becomes antiquated... unless they teach theory. I'm sure most of the older teachers out there are learning or first hearing about new technology from their students. Most students these days don't have the time, patience or financial resources to learn about why. It's more about the "show me how", and now. The students who want to learn about the why are seeking a deeper understanding. They will be the future graduate students. But those students will be looking for work that the "show me how" BA students went out and secured already.

Is it King Ludd again – are they burning the factories so that the work cannot be automated?

This question has to do with the time in England when the weaving industry turned towards automation. This disruption quickly diminished the amount of "weavers" needed - this was for a major occupation at the time. The legend goes that the displaced "weavers" would go around at night and burn down the factories that adopted the new technology. Since no one knew who was actually doing the destruction the name of King Ludd was thrown out.

This is where we get the term "Luddite". See article excerpt from The National Archives England –

"Who were the Luddites and what did they want?

The machine-breaking disturbances that rocked the wool and cotton industries were known as the 'Luddite riots'. The Luddites were named after 'General Ned Ludd' or 'King Ludd', a mythical figure who lived in Sherwood Forest and supposedly led the movement.

They began in Nottinghamshire in 1811 and quickly spread throughout the country, especially to the West Riding of Yorkshire and Lancashire in 1812, and also to Leicestershire and Derbyshire. In Yorkshire, they wanted to get rid of the new machinery that was causing unemployment among workers. Hand weavers did not want the introduction of power looms. In Nottinghamshire, they protested against wage reductions.

Workers sent threatening letters to employers and broke into factories to destroy the new machines, such as the new wide weaving frames. They also attacked employers, magistrates and food merchants. There were fights between Luddites and government soldiers.

http://www.nationalarchives.gov.uk/education/politics/g3/

Is this what is happening today? Are educators purposely turning away and discrediting the use of technology in the classroom as insufficient and unusable to basically "burn the factories"? Here is a bit from an article by Neil Selwyn on academia.edu.

Perhaps the most pervasive example of these re-schooling discourses has been the notion of 'twenty-first century skills' – a recurring feature of educational technology debate around the world. 'Twenty-first century skills' is now an accepted description of the required skill-sets, competencies, pedagogies, curricular and assessment reforms and systemic arrangements that are seen to necessitate education reform – quite simply a blueprint for education in a digital age. While descriptions of these 'twenty-first century skills' may vary, the underlying imperatives remain the same – i.e. changing the structures, processes and practices of schools, teachers and students along more high-tech, networked and 'innovative' lines. –

Along with other further reasoning and beliefs.

De-schooling discourses have long persisted within discussions of digital education. Indeed, a subtle rejectionist line of thinking is apparent throughout the arguments of Seymour Papert – perhaps the founding father of academic educational technology. Papert was fond of asserting along lines that "the computer will blow up the school"(Papert 1984, p.38), or new technology will "overthrow the accepted structure of school... and pretty well

everything that the education establishment will defend to the bitter end"
(Papert 1998, n.p.).

These bon mots have been repeated frequently and with much approval in educational technology circles, and over three decades on continue to be an accepted part of mainstream thinking about education and technology. Now, many commentators are willing to denounce formal educational institutions as 'anachronistic' relics of the industrial age that are now rendered obsolete by contemporary digital technology. As Suoranta and Vadén (2010, p.16) conclude: "in their current forms it might be that schools not longer belong to the order of things in the late modern era, and are about to vanish from the map of human affairs" - http://www.academia.edu/4147878/Discourses_of_digital_disruption_in_e ducation_a_critical_analysis

What will happen economically to the nation if the educational institutions do not modify the curriculum to a STEM or STEAM based curriculum?

Well according to a recent study done by the White House entitled:

"The President's Council of Advisors on Science and Technology

Executive Report

Prepare and Inspire: K-12 Science, Technology, Engineering, and Math (STEM)

Education for America's Future"

Troubling Signs

"Despite our historical record of achievement, the United States now lags behind other nations in STEM education at the elementary and secondary levels. International comparisons of our students' performance in science and mathematics consistently place the United States in the middle of the pack or lower. On the National Assessment of Educational Progress, less than one-third of U.S. eighth graders show proficiency in mathematics and science."

According to the same study a focus by educational institutions on STEM or STEAM based curriculum the following should occur.

"(4) EDUCATIONAL TECHNOLOGY: USE TECHNOLOGY TO DRIVE INNOVATION, BY CREATING AN ADVANCED RESEARCH PROJECTS AGENCY FOR EDUCATION

Information and computation technology can be a powerful driving force for innovation in education, by improving the quality of instructional materials available to teachers and students, aiding in the development of high-quality assessments that capture student learning, and accelerating the collection and use of data to provide rich feedback to students, teachers, and schools. Moreover, technology has been advancing rapidly to the point that it can soon play a transformative role in education." - *http://www.whitehouse.gov/sites/default/files/microsites/ostp/pcast-stemed-report.pdf*

And where it has been embraced and put into action these are some results.

"The passions for science, mathematics, engineering, and art are driven by the same desire: the desire to discover the beauty in one's world," notes Virginia Malone, a retired senior science project director in Hondo, Texas. "Art is also integrated into technologies as engineers go from crude designs to finished products...From model T Ford to the latest concept car, we see the evolution of technology is as much about aesthetics of the product as its functionality." -
http://www.nsta.org/publications/news/story.aspx?id=56924

"For both sites, the underlying message is the same: These projects opened doors to opportunities and partnerships that were previously beyond reach for the communities they impact, and it is ultimately the strong value of the work to students, schools, and communities that will keep it going in the future."-
http://www.neafoundation.org/content/assets/2012/08/nea_stemreport_final-5.pdf

Chapter 10 - P.S.

Get it "PostScript" – nerd humor.

To me the main question of all that has been written about is this...

It is 2015. We are one-seventh the way through this new millennium and over fifty years since the birth of the Internet. When are we going to embrace these major shifts? What will it take to move forward? Why can't we as a society see that what we are doing by holding back this new Digital Incunabula is creating a failed structure in the terms of information, publishing, promotion, entertainment, education and the arts? Why haven't we learned that not changing the core of how we live, teach and work towards a new global effort will push us far off the world stage?

Here are some forecasts for 2015 and beyond on STEM, STEAM and Applied Theory:

Gartner Predicts Top 2015 And Beyond Trends For Technology, IT Organizations, And Consumers

By 2018, Gartner predicts, digital business will require 50% less business process workers and 500% more key digital business jobs, compared with traditional models. The top jobs for digital over the next seven years will be:

- *Integration Specialists*

- *Digital Business Architects*

- *Regulatory Analysts*

- *Risk Professionals*

Gartner: "You must build talent for the digital organization of 2020 now. Not just the digital technology organization, but the whole enterprise. Talent is the key to digital leadership." –

http://www.forbes.com/sites/gilpress/2014/10/09/gartner-predicts-top-trends-for-technology-it-organizations-and-consumers-for-2015-and-beyond/2/

"As was noted at the recent U.S. News STEM Leadership Summit in Dallas, a crisis exists and Americans must act now to address the gap in jobs and available talent. Estimates show the U.S. will have over 1.2 million unfilled jobs in science, technology, engineering, and math by 2018. The crisis we face pits these unfilled jobs against a population that is not qualified or prepared to do them." - http://www.usnews.com/news/blogs/stem-education/2012/08/15/industry-educators-build-in-roads-to-stem-success

"The Applied Theory Initiative was established at the University of Chicago Booth School of Business in January 2009. The primary purpose of the initiative is to bring together faculty from a variety of disciplines including accounting, behavioral science, economics, finance, marketing, operations and political science whose research makes use of similar theoretical tools in:

- *Optimization*
- *Incentives*
- *Price Theory*
- *Game Theory*

To this end, the Applied Theory Initiative promotes two programs. First, the Workshop on Applied Theory, is a weekly seminar during the Fall and Spring Quarters that features both internal and external researchers working on significant topics in applied theory. Second, a year-round Visiting Fellows program hosts several week-long visits from applied theorists outside the University of Chicago who are leaders in their respective fields." - http://faculty.chicagobooth.edu/appliedtheory/about.html

This is why I push so hard for the "why", not only the "how. But this time, why am I so concerned? Because this time the ripples are hitting the shore hard, because this time there is great chaos surrounding us, because this time the waves are crashing around us from all angles, because this time to paraphrase Robert Duvall in "Apocalypse Now" - "We all better surf".

Now here is the biggest question – If you were going to advise a child as to how to invest in their future what would you choose now?

Now let's make it personal – if you were to advise YOUR child as to how to invest in their future what would you choose now?

Everyday I try to help answer that question.

And that is what I love about teaching.

P.P.S.

So here goes my one and only recommendation for students, parents and anyone getting started or changing a career.

It comes from the 1967 movie the "Graduate" and it always plays through my mind as it did with Negroponte's quote. The advice given to Benjamin Braddock, Dustin Hoffman, was...

"Plastics."

"Exactly how do you mean?" asked Ben.

"There's a great future in plastics," replied Mr. McGuire.

"Think about it. Will you think about it?"

But there is a great future in "Glass"

and "Titanium"

...or whatever material your device is made of

That device holds your entrance into a digital world, just get involved, know "how" it works and "why" it works, so you can create the next one or simply the work that goes on it, because you actually DO hold your future in your hand... everyday.

Just try not to butt dial it.

Bibliography

"10 Worst College Majors for Your Career." *Www.kiplinger.com*. N.p., n.d. Web. 21
  Oct. 2015. <http://www.kiplinger.com/slideshow/college/T012-S001-
  worst-college-majors-for-your-career-2015-
  2016/index.html#3TKYLolB4ms2mCZ2.99>.

"11 Innovations That Changed History." *History.com*. A&E Television Networks,
  n.d. Web. 21 Oct. 2015. <http://www.history.com/news/history-lists/11-
  innovations-that-changed-history>.

"2012 - Changing Course: Ten Years of Tracking Online Education in the United
  States - OLC." *OLC*. N.p., n.d. Web. 21 Oct. 2015.
  <http://onlinelearningconsortium.org/survey_report/changing-course-
  ten-years-tracking-online-education-united-states/>.

"About | Ben Fry." *About | Ben Fry*. N.p., n.d. Web. 21 Oct. 2015.
  <http://benfry.com/about/>.

"About the Standards." *Common Core State Standards Initiative About the Standards Comments*. N.p., n.d. Web. 21 Oct. 2015.
  <http://www.corestandards.org/about-the-standards/>.

"Accenture | Strategy, Consulting, Digital, Technology and Operations." *Accenture |
  Strategy, Consulting, Digital, Technology and Operations*. N.p., n.d. Web. 21
  Oct. 2015. <http://www.accenture.com/us-en/outlook/Pages/outlook-
  journal-2013-long-view-digital-disruption.aspx>.

Allen, Jesmond, and James Chudley. *Smashing UX Design: Foundations for Designing Online User Experiences*. Chichester, West Sussex: John Wiley & Sons, 2012. Print.

"The American Newspaper Media Industry Revenue Profile 2012." *The American Newspaper Media Industry Revenue Profile 2012*. N.p., n.d. Web. 21 Oct. 2015. <http://www.naa.org/trends-and-numbers/newspaper-revenue/newspaper-media-industry-revenue-profile-2012.aspx>.

"AmplifyÂ¬ ." *Amplify Announces New Tablet Designed by IntelÂ® Education*. N.p., n.d. Web. 21 Oct. 2015. <http://www.amplify.com/newsroom/press-release/amplify-intel>.

"Art In America." *The Museum Interface*. N.p., n.d. Web. 21 Oct. 2015. <http://www.artinamericamagazine.com/news-features/magazine/the-museum-interface/>.

"The Art, Technology, and Culture Colloquium." *UC Berkeley Art, Technology, and Culture Colloquium*. N.p., n.d. Web. 21 Oct. 2015. <http://atc.berkeley.edu/bio/Camille_Utterback/>.

"Art/Museums: The 2002 Biennial at the Whitney Museum of American Art." *Art/Museums: The 2002 Biennial at the Whitney Museum of American Art*. N.p., n.d. Web. 21 Oct. 2015. <http://www.thecityreview.com/biennial.html>.

"Artport." *Artport*. N.p., n.d. Web. 21 Oct. 2015. <http://whitney.org/Exhibitions/Artport>.

Barnes, Brooks. "Movies Have Worst Summer Since 1997." *The New York Times*. The New York Times, 29 Aug. 2014. Web. 21 Oct. 2015. <http://www.nytimes.com/2014/08/30/movies/movies-have-worst-summer-since-1997.html?_r=0>.

Bio.com. A&E Networks Television, n.d. Web. 21 Oct. 2015. <http://www.biography.com/people/elon-musk-20837159>.

"Books & Resources." *NSTA News*. N.p., n.d. Web. 21 Oct. 2015. <http://www.nsta.org/publications/news/story.aspx?id=56924>.

"Books & Resources." *NSTA News*. N.p., n.d. Web. 21 Oct. 2015. <http://www.nsta.org/publications/news/story.aspx?id=59305>.

"The Changing Textbook Industry - Disruptive Competition Project." *Disruptive Competition Project*. N.p., 21 Nov. 2013. Web. 21 Oct. 2015. <http://www.project-disco.org/competition/112113-the-changing-textbook-industry/>.

Cotter, Holland. "Spiritual America, From Ecstatic To Transcendent." *The New York Times*. The New York Times, 07 Mar. 2002. Web. 21 Oct. 2015. <http://www.nytimes.com/2002/03/08/arts/art-review-spiritual-america-from-ecstatic-to-transcendent.html>.

Cox, John Woodrow. "Tablets on the Rise in Nation's Schools." *Washington Post*. The Washington Post, n.d. Web. 21 Oct. 2015. <http://www.washingtonpost.com/local/education/tablets-proliferate-in-nations-classrooms-and-take-a-swipe-at-the-status-quo/2014/05/17/faa27ba4-dbbd-11e3-8009-71de85b9c527_story.html>.

"Design Takes Over, Says Paola Antonelli." *The Economist*. The Economist Newspaper, 22 Nov. 2010. Web. 21 Oct. 2015. <http://www.economist.com/node/17509367>.

"The Digital Degree." *The Economist*. The Economist Newspaper, 28 June 2014. Web. 21 Oct. 2015. <http://www.economist.com/news/briefing/21605899-staid-higher-education-business-about-experience-welcome-earthquake-digital>.

"Discourses of Digital 'disruption' in Education: A Critical Analysis." *Discourses of Digital 'disruption' in Education: A Critical Analysis*. N.p., n.d. Web. 21 Oct. 2015. <http://www.academia.edu/4147878/Discourses_of_digital_disruption_in_education_a_critical_analysis>.

"Disney Interactive Slashes 700 Jobs." *Animation Magazine RSS*. N.p., 06 Mar. 2014. Web. 21 Oct. 2015. <http://www.animationmagazine.net/top-stories/disney-interactive-slashes-700-jobs/>.

"Disruptions: Design Rivals Technology in Importance." *Bits Disruptions Design Rivals Technology in Importance Comments*. N.p., 13 Jan. 2013. Web. 21 Oct. 2015. <http://bits.blogs.nytimes.com/2013/01/13/disruptions-design-to-propel-technology-forward/?_r=0>.

E., Executive Office Of The President, President'S Council Of Advisors On, and Science And Technology. (n.d.): n. pag. Web.

"Ebooks v Paper - FT.com." *Financial Times*. N.p., n.d. Web. 21 Oct. 2015. <http://www.ft.com/cms/s/2/53d3096a-f792-11e3-90fa-00144feabdc0.html>.

"Economic Outlook for the U.S. Printing and Publishing Industry." - *Springer*. N.p., 01 Sept. 1996. Web. 21 Oct. 2015. <http://link.springer.com/article/10.1007/BF02680366>.

"Effectively Planning UX Design Projects – Smashing Magazine." *Smashing Magazine*. N.p., 24 Jan. 2013. Web. 21 Oct. 2015. <http://www.smashingmagazine.com/2013/01/effectively-planning-ux-design-projects/>.

"Effectively Planning UX Design Projects – Smashing Magazine." *Smashing Magazine*. N.p., 24 Jan. 2013. Web. 21 Oct. 2015. <http://www.smashingmagazine.com/2013/01/effectively-planning-ux-design-projects/>.

"EXHIBITIONS." *MoMA*. N.p., n.d. Web. 21 Oct. 2015.
      <http://www.moma.org/visit/calendar/exhibitions/1080>.

"FindLaw's New York Supreme Court Case and Opinions." *Findlaw*. N.p., n.d. Web.
      21 Oct. 2015. <http://caselaw.findlaw.com/ny-supreme-
      court/1170198.html>.

Forbes. Forbes Magazine, n.d. Web. 21 Oct. 2015.
      <http://www.forbes.com/sites/gilpress/2014/10/09/gartner-predicts-
      top-trends-for-technology-it-organizations-and-consumers-for-2015-
      and-beyond/2/>.

"Gen-i:The Rise of Generation Interactive | OnEnterFrame." *OnEnterFrame*. N.p.,
      n.d. Web. 21 Oct. 2015. <http://patrickaievoli.com/gen-ithe-rise-of-
      generation-interactive/>.

"Genius or Process? How Top Creative Directors Come Up With Great Ideas."
      AdWeek. N.p., n.d. Web. 21 Oct. 2015.
      <http://www.adweek.com/news/advertising-branding/genius-or-
      process-how-top-creative-directors-come-great-ideas-152697>.

"Google Defeats Authors in U.S. Book-scanning Lawsuit." *Reuters*. Thomson Reu-
      ters, 14 Nov. 2013. Web. 21 Oct. 2015.
      <http://www.reuters.com/article/2013/11/14/us-google-books-
      idUSBRE9AD0TT20131114>.

"Groundbreaking Research." N.p., n.d. Web. 21 Oct. 2015.
      <http://mitsloan.mit.edu/ide/research/>.

"Guggenheim." *YouTube Play*. N.p., n.d. Web. 21 Oct. 2015.
      <http://www.guggenheim.org/new-york/online/participate/youtube-
      play>.

Heller, Steven. "Down to the Letters." *The New York Times*. The New York Times,
      20 Oct. 2012. Web. 21 Oct. 2015.
      <http://www.nytimes.com/2012/10/21/books/review/graphic-design-
      before-graphic-designers-and-more.html?pagewanted=all&_r=1>.

HernÁndez, Javier C. "Common Core, in 9-Year-Old Eyes." *The New York Times*. The
      New York Times, 14 June 2014. Web. 21 Oct. 2015.
      <http://www.nytimes.com/2014/06/15/education/common-core-in-9-
      year-old-eyes.html?_r=0>.

"The History of 3D Printing - Redorbit." *Redorbit*. N.p., n.d. Web. 21 Oct. 2015.
      <http://www.redorbit.com/education/reference_library/general-
      2/history-of/1112953506/the-history-of-3d-
      printing/#wz983px6VlLE75hz.99>.

"IAB.com." *IAB.com*. N.p., n.d. Web. 21 Oct. 2015.
      <http://www.iab.net/about_the_iab/recent_press_releases/press_release
      _archive/press_release/pr-102014#sthash.Bb7ehQHa.dpuf>.

"Ideo's David Kelley on "Design Thinking"" *Fast Company.* N.p., 01 Feb. 2009. Web. 21 Oct. 2015. <http://www.fastcompany.com/1139331/ideos-david-kelley-design-thinking>.

"Internet Hall of Fame." *Timeline.* N.p., n.d. Web. 21 Oct. 2015. <http://www.internethalloffame.org/internet-history/timeline>.

"Internet History 1962 to 1992." *Internet History 1962 to 1992.* N.p., n.d. Web. 21 Oct. 2015. <http://www.computerhistory.org/internet_history/>.

"It's Time to Start Taking Pinterest Seriously." *Daily Intelligencer.* N.p., 24 Oct. 2013. Web. 21 Oct. 2015. <http://nymag.com/daily/intelligencer/2013/10/time-to-start-taking-pinterest-seriously.html>.

"Kodak Files for Bankruptcy as Digital Era Spells End to Film." *Bloomberg.com.* Bloomberg, n.d. Web. 21 Oct. 2015. <http://www.bloomberg.com/news/articles/2012-01-19/kodak-photography-pioneer-files-for-bankruptcy-protection-1->.

Levin, David. "Dear Students and Faculty: Please Go Digital." *The Huffington Post.* TheHuffingtonPost.com, n.d. Web. 21 Oct. 2015. <http://www.huffingtonpost.com/david-levin/dear-students-and-faculty_b_7957508.html>.

"Meet the 2014 CNBC Disruptor 50 Company List." *CNBC.* N.p., 17 June 2014. Web. 21 Oct. 2015. <http://www.cnbc.com/id/101734664>.

"Michael Lewis Explains His Book "Flash Boys"" *CBSNews.* CBS Interactive, n.d. Web. 21 Oct. 2015. <http://www.cbsnews.com/news/michael-lewis-explains-his-book-flash-boys/>.

Miller, Claire Cain, and Julie Bosman. "E-Books Outsell Print Books at Amazon." *The New York Times.* The New York Times, 19 May 2011. Web. 21 Oct. 2015.

"Mooc.ca." ~ *MOOC.* N.p., n.d. Web. 21 Oct. 2015. <http://www.mooc.ca/providers.htm>.

"Neil Young, Jack White Cut Vinyl Record Live on 'Tonight Show'" *Rolling Stone.* N.p., 13 May 2014. Web. 21 Oct. 2015. <http://www.rollingstone.com/music/videos/neil-young-jack-white-cut-vinyl-record-live-on-tonight-show-20140513#ixzz3Op8rHqvI>.

"New." *MFA Interaction Design, SVA.* N.p., n.d. Web. 21 Oct. 2015. <http://interactiondesign.sva.edu/>.

"Newspapers: Revenue from Retail, National and Classified Ads (2013)." *Pew Research Centers Journalism Project RSS.* N.p., 25 Mar. 2014. Web. 21 Oct. 2015. <http://www.journalism.org/media-indicators/newspaper-revenue-from-retail-national-and-classified-ads/>.

"Newswire ." *How Social Media Impacts Brand Marketing*. N.p., n.d. Web. 21 Oct. 2015. <http://www.nielsen.com/us/en/insights/news/2011/how-social-media-impacts-brand-marketing.html>.

"Nicholas Negroponte | MIT Media Lab." *Nicholas Negroponte | MIT Media Lab*. N.p., n.d. Web. 21 Oct. 2015. <http://www.media.mit.edu/people/nicholas>.

"NY School Goes All-in on Digital Textbooks - NBC News." *NBC News*. N.p., n.d. Web. 21 Oct. 2015. <http://www.nbcnews.com/business/business-news/ny-school-goes-all-digital-textbooks-f2D11792419>.

"Our Point of View." *Dschool*. N.p., n.d. Web. 21 Oct. 2015. <http://dschool.stanford.edu/our-point-of-view/#design-thinking>.

Pappano, Laura. "The Year of the MOOC." *The New York Times*. The New York Times, 03 Nov. 2012. Web. 21 Oct. 2015. <http://www.nytimes.com/2012/11/04/education/edlife/massive-open-online-courses-are-multiplying-at-a-rapid-pace.html?pagewanted=all&_r=0>.

"Paywalls Versus Advertising? Why Not Both? - Folio:." *Folio*. N.p., 10 June 2011. Web. 21 Oct. 2015. <http://www.foliomag.com/2011/paywalls-versus-advertising-why-not-both/>.

Pfanner, Eric. "Music Industry Sales Rise, and Digital Revenue Gets the Credit." *The New York Times*. The New York Times, 26 Feb. 2013. Web. 21 Oct. 2015. <http://www.nytimes.com/2013/02/27/technology/music-industry-records-first-revenue-increase-since-1999.html?_r=0>.

Popova, Maria. "Analog Graphic Design to Die For: 5 Fantastic Die-Cut Books." *The Atlantic*. Atlantic Media Company, 29 Aug. 2011. Web. 21 Oct. 2015. <http://www.theatlantic.com/entertainment/archive/2011/08/analog-graphic-design-to-die-for-5-fantastic-die-cut-books/244272/>.

"Printing in the US: Market Research Report." *Printing in the US Market Research*. N.p., n.d. Web. 21 Oct. 2015. <http://www.ibisworld.com/industry/default.aspx?indid=433>.

Report, The Nea Foundation, and Www.neafoundation.org. *Harnessing the Potential of Innovative STEM Education Programs: Stories of Collaboration, Connectedness and Empowerment* (n.d.): n. pag. Web.

Report, The Nea Foundation. *Harnessing the Potential of Innovative STEM Education Programs: Stories of Collaboration, Connectedness and Empowerment* (n.d.): n. pag. Web.

"Rhizome | Margot Lovejoy." *Rhizome | Margot Lovejoy*. N.p., n.d. Web. 21 Oct. 2015. <http://rhizome.org/profiles/margotlovejoy/>.

Robinson, Ken, and Lou Aronica. *The Element: How Finding Your Passion Changes Everything*. New York: Viking, 2009. Print.

Robinson, Sir Ken. "Transform Education? Yes, We Must." *The Huffington Post*. TheHuffingtonPost.com, n.d. Web. 21 Oct. 2015. <http://www.huffingtonpost.com/sir-ken-robinson/transform-education-yes-w_b_157014.html>.

"SFMOMA | SFMOMA | Exhibitions + Events | Calendar | E.space | Mark Napier." *San Francisco Museum of Modern Art*. N.p., n.d. Web. 21 Oct. 2015.

"Should Tech Designers Go With Their Guts — Or the Data?" *Wired.com*. Conde Nast Digital, n.d. Web. 21 Oct. 2015. <http://www.wired.com/2013/11/design-world-stop-fighting-over-data-vs-instinct/>.

Since the Introduction the ITunes Music Store on April 28. "A Decade of ITunes Singles Killed the Music Industry." *CNNMoney*. Cable News Network, n.d. Web. 21 Oct. 2015. <http://money.cnn.com/2013/04/25/technology/itunes-music-decline/>.

"So You Want to Be an Interaction Designer." *Cooper*. N.p., n.d. Web. 21 Oct. 2015. <http://www.cooper.com/journal/2008/05/so_you_want_to_be_an_inter acti>.

"Solutions ." *Nielsen Digital Ad Ratings*. N.p., n.d. Web. 21 Oct. 2015. <http://www.nielsen.com/campaignratings.html>.

"State of the News Media 2014." *Pew Research Centers Journalism Project RSS*. N.p., 25 Mar. 2014. Web. 21 Oct. 2015. <http://www.journalism.org/2014/03/26/state-of-the-news-media-2014-overview/>.

"Taking the Learning Tablets." *The Economist*. The Economist Newspaper, 07 June 2014. Web. 21 Oct. 2015. <http://www.economist.com/news/international/21603471-latest-innovations-promise-big-improvements-teaching-taking-learning-tablets>.

"Top 10 IPad and IPhone Paper-Replacement Apps." *TechHive*. N.p., n.d. Web. 21 Oct. 2015. <http://www.techhive.com/article/241198/top_10_ipad_and_iphone_pa per_replacement_apps.html>.

"A Tough Lesson for College Textbook Publishers." *WSJ*. N.p., n.d. Web. 21 Oct. 2015. <http://www.wsj.com/articles/a-tough-lesson-for-college-textbook-publishers-1409182139>.

"The Trouble With 'Viewability' as a Metric for Digital Ads." *Advertising Age DigitalNext RSS*. N.p., n.d. Web. 21 Oct. 2015. <http://adage.com/article/digitalnext/trouble-viewability-a-metric-digital-ads/237815/>.

"US TV-advert Buyers Hold Back as Viewers Move Online - FT.com." *Financial Times*. N.p., n.d. Web. 21 Oct. 2015. <http://www.ft.com/cms/s/0/edf1df26-2a32-11e4-8139-00144feabdc0.html#ixzz3Op2GohNX>.

Wall, Mike. "Space Stationu0027s 3D Printer Makes Wrench From U0027Beamed Upu0027 Design | Space.com." N.p., n.d. Web. 21 Oct. 2015. <http://www.space.com/28095-3d-printer-space-station-ratchet-wrench.html>.

"The Whitney's Digital Sampler." *NYMag.com*. N.p., n.d. Web. 21 Oct. 2015. <http://nymag.com/nymetro/arts/features/4507/>.

"Why John Maeda Is Leaving RISD For A Venture Capital Firm." *Co.Design*. N.p., 06 Dec. 2013. Web. 21 Oct. 2015. <http://www.fastcodesign.com/3023047/why-john-maeda-is-leaving-risd-for-a-venture-capital-firm>.

Wikipedia. Wikimedia Foundation, n.d. Web. 21 Oct. 2015. <http://en.wikipedia.org/wiki/Being_Digital>.

"William Hess (johnmaeda) on About.me." *About.me*. N.p., n.d. Web. 21 Oct. 2015. <http://about.me/johnmaeda>.

"William Hess (johnmaeda) on About.me." *About.me*. N.p., n.d. Web. 21 Oct. 2015. <http://about.me/johnmaeda>.

Winograd, Terry. *Bringing Design to Software*. New York, NY: ACM, 1996. Print.

"WIRED 3.01 - Bits and Atoms." *WIRED 3.01 - Bits and Atoms*. N.p., n.d. Web. 21 Oct. 2015. <http://web.media.mit.edu/~nicholas/Wired/WIRED3-01.html>.

"Wired 6.12: Negroponte." *Wired 6.12: Negroponte*. N.p., n.d. Web. 21 Oct. 2015. <http://archive.wired.com/wired/archive/6.12/negroponte.html>.

"With Few Blockbusters, Hollywood's Summer Box Office Revenues Drop - The Portland Press Herald / Maine Sunday Telegram." *The Portland Press Herald Maine Sunday Telegram With Few Blockbusters Hollywoods Summer Box Office Revenues Drop Comments*. N.p., 09 July 2014. Web. 21 Oct. 2015. <http://www.pressherald.com/2014/07/10/with-few-blockbusters-hollywoods-summer-box-office-revenues-drop/>.

About the author

Patrick Aievoli started his career in 1978 as a designer for local editorial and advertising companies. In 1984, he became a promotional designer at McGraw-Hill. Professor Aievoli has been a full-time academic since 1989 when he left his position as senior designer, print promotion, at the McGraw-Hill Book Company. During his time at McGraw-Hill Patrick helped in the creation of McGraw-Hill's first interactive CD-ROM "Encyclopedia of Science and Technology" in 1987.

In 1990 to 1996 Prof. Aievoli completed his thesis on "The Use of New Media in Higher Education" culminating in an interactive art history CD-ROM featuring core and dynamic content along with a simplified suite of online learning tools.

In 1998 he became a full-time faculty member at LIU Post in Brookville, NY. He became the director of the campus' Interactive Multimedia Arts graduate program in 1999 and has built the program since the start.

Although he is a dedicated academic, Professor Aievoli is still involved in the new media arena and has consulted for some of the metro area's largest new media companies.

Academic Experience

Associate Professor

Director of the Interactive Multimedia Arts graduate program

Long Island University Post campus

Brookville, New York.

Teaching full time at the college level for the past 27 years, responsible for hiring, budget, recruitment, promotion, technology and advisement.

Course development and teaching experience include the following;

Interactive design/ Digital imaging – Adobe Creative Suite,

Digital video/audio – Final Cut/Premiere/After Effects

Curriculum development – Digital Game Design undergraduate LIU Post

Served on development committee and search committee for program

USDAN Center for the Arts – developed digital game design program for 8 – 15 year olds

- **Client Roster (Partial)**
- Directly involved in the conception, creation and final production of numerous new media projects for companies such as:
- American Express
- Association for Computing Machinery
- Autism Academy
- Computer Sales Specialists
- Electro Dynamics, Inc.
- FleetBoston,
- LinuxIDG
- McGraw-Hill Health Professions
- New York Islanders
- Verizon/NYNEX
- TimeWarner/SONY
- Tommy HilfigerUSA

Awards

- Long Island Business News – "50 over 50" - 2010
- 6 Time Long Island Advertising Club - Advisor for Student Best On Long Island winner 2002, 2003, 2004, 2006, 2008 and 2009
- How Magazine Award – 1996

Publications:

- "on enterFrame", 2008, Whittier Publications, Long Beach, NY
- "Support the Aesthetic through Metaphorical Thinking", 2004,
  Journal of National Collegiate Honors Council
- "Colliding Forces", Chapter "Collide", 2004, McNabb and Kremer, Kendall Hunt

Speaking engagements:

- Seybold Seminars, 1996, 1997, 2000, 2002
- Acxiom Direct Marketing conference, 1999

Adjudication for academic and industry shows:

- Knowledge Industry Publications (KIP) Top 100 Multimedia Producers 1999-2000
- Long Island Media Arts Juried Exhibition 1999-2008

The University of Nebraska–Lincoln does not discriminate based on gender, age, disability, race, color, religion, marital status, veteran's status, national or ethnic origin, or sexual orientation.

www.ingramcontent.com/pod-product-compliance
Lightning Source LLC
Chambersburg PA
CBHW051249050326
40689CB00007B/1120